BESHARAM
बेशरम

PRIYA-ALIKA ELIAS

BESHARAM
बेशरम

*On Love
and Other
Bad
Behaviors*

CHICAGO
REVIEW
PRESS

Published by Chicago Review Press Incorporated
814 North Franklin Street
Chicago, Illinois 60610
ISBN 978-1-64160-507-6

First published by Penguin Random House India Private Limited

Cover design: Sadie Teper
Front cover image: Kristina Petrick
Typeset in Adobe Caslon Pro by Manipal Digital Systems, Manipal

Printed in the United States of America
5 4 3 2 1

To my mother and father, for loving me and never asking too many questions. Thank you, thank you, thank you.

Contents

BESHARAM
बेशरम

I
SEX

Shameless

I wonder what men feel when they buy condoms.

Stand-up comics often joke about this: the singularly male experience of the humblebrag. "You feel embarrassed," they grin, "but you also feel cool. It's like announcing to the world, '*Look at me, I'm about to have sex.*'"

The humblebrag, of course, is not a part of the rich package of emotions available to women. (A woman is either bragging—I lost weight on the keto diet, I got a promotion at work![1]—or she's being humble, as she ought to be.) More importantly, the act of buying condoms as a woman is not a brag at all. As men frequently remind us, women can have sex whenever we please. They trot out their favorite lock-and-key metaphors to keep us in our place. We are the gatekeepers of morality, and what sort of gatekeeper would brag about buying condoms? Only a *bad* one.

Like many Indian women, I was something of a late bloomer sexually. While the boys in my class were already watching "blue" films and masturbating vigorously in groups, I stayed at home and read long books. Thus, I was eighteen and still a virgin when my friend asked me to buy the morning-after pill for her.

"I'll wait here," she said, handing me the money in Khan Market. "It's the shop right there."

I asked, "why can't you buy it?" reasonably.

"I don't want to. Please."

I thought she was being ridiculous, but I went in anyway. There was a man at the counter and two others in the shop, stacking boxes of complicated-sounding pills.

"The morning-after pill, please," I said.

Have you ever said something and felt the atmosphere in the room change? The very people in it transform from languid to watchful?

"Unwanted-72?"

I couldn't believe they called it that. *Unwanted.* It gave the transaction the seediness of a late-term abortion. I imagined somebody flinging a 90 percent-formed baby into the garbage heap, when in fact it had only been a few hours ago that my friend had had ill-advised sex.

He pushed the package across the counter and took my 100-rupee note, staring at me in a way that he had not permitted himself before. The other men neglected their box-piling duties to watch me walk out of the shop. I felt a hot shame but also a sense of defiance: why should I not buy the morning-after pill? At that moment, I imagined that I was the one who'd had sex, that it was my idiot boyfriend who had forgotten to buy condoms, that I was now announcing myself to the world as a haver of sex. If I couldn't humble-brag, at least I could defiant-brag.

* * *

"*Log kya kahenge?*"

It is cliché, that cry. By now, we have all heard it in so many Bollywood movies, in so many jokes and send-ups of desi culture that we are bored. And yet, no matter how many times we hear it, no matter how many casual comments we make about *not caring what people think*, we are not free of its tyranny.

People spend a lot of time thinking about Indian women having sex. This much is undeniable. There is a curious eroticism even to the good Indian woman, submissive and silent. Boys all over India masturbate to "aunties" ("aunty" being one of the most popular search terms in India[2]). Neighboring aunty. MILF. *Bhabhi* with young brother-in-law. Stepmother with stepson. The women in these videos have nothing in common with the glossy, perfect porn stars on Brazzers. Instead, they look much more like the tired women we see in our kitchens, wiping one atta-smeared hand across their foreheads. Perhaps, it is precisely for that reason that they are more popular with young, hot-blooded Indian men.

And yet we stubbornly and steadfastly refuse to talk about sex. To bring it into the public domain. Sex is something that happens quickly under bedsheets, or covertly in the afternoon while the children are playing and you're pretending to have your afternoon nap. It happens after marriage for purposes of procreation, because *those things are not in our culture.*

The only people who talk about sex are men (often making what they call "non-vegetarian jokes" to other men). Growing up, I never encountered raucous women like the ones on *Sex and the City*, who spent Sundays at restaurants discussing their partners' sexual fortitude. I didn't even know what counted as sexual activity, or which types of sexual activity could lead to pregnancy. (I didn't have one of those glossy American books called *Your Body and You* to explain those mysterious dynamics, those hormonal shifts.) Could you get pregnant from kissing? In my confused adolescent imagination, you could.

"You'll have to be careful now," my grandmother told me when she saw the bloodstains on my bed. (I had just awoken from a sweaty nap, and I regarded them with wonder—nobody had told me about periods.) "You're a woman now, and you must cross your legs when you sit, and not run around with the colony boys playing cricket. Those days are over."

Although I have a younger brother, I understood as if by instinct that he would receive no such warning. Oh, he would go through the rituals of puberty—the first sign of stubble on his cheeks, the deepening of his still-babyish voice—but there was nothing in his future that had to change. Maybe this is the saddest thing about being a woman: attaining womanhood means learning what we are forbidden to do. Attaining manhood means learning what you are capable of.

When I first read "Girl" by Jamaica Kincaid, I shivered with recognition. Although Kincaid was writing of an entirely different cultural context—the island nation of Antigua in the 1980s—I knew that the contours and textures of her world were similar to mine. "On Sundays, try to walk like a lady and not like the slut you are so bent on becoming," intones the mother figure in a mournful voice to the carefree young girl who is the subject of the short story. "Don't squat down to play marbles—you are not a boy, you know [. . .]."

For the girl, growing up is an act of learning. She is taught how to cook, how to clean, and how to be a woman. The boy, meanwhile, plays cricket in the garden. His world is still unlimited.

I thought of the Malayalam proverb: *Ila mullil veenalum mullu ilayil veenalum, ilaykanu dosham* (whether a leaf falls on the thorn or a thorn on a leaf, it is the leaf that will suffer). It is us, always us, who must suffer. It is a proverb repeated to wanton women to remind them of what can happen.

The very word "shameless" is deeply gendered. How many men have you heard being called shameless? It may be jokingly applied, but it is difficult to think of a man who has been adjudged "besharam" in all seriousness. No no, besharam is for women who want things, who are fearless about voicing those wants, who are frankly unapologetic about it.

In such a context, with such a childhood, how will women speak about sex or desire? If the Internet is to be believed, Indian men are absolutely stuffed to the gills with desire. "Nice bobs mam," "very nyc dear," "kiss to u" are the comments they leave on popular female celebrities' pages. They message women they've never met on Facebook, asking if they can "make frandship." This is so ubiquitous as to have become a meme: even Americans know that "show bobs and vagene" is likely to have come from a horny man sitting in front of a computer somewhere in India. These are the men so desirous that they keep and share logs of WhatsApp numbers that they believe belong to women.

But, where are the women?

* * *

"Good girls don't."

The ideal Indian woman is clearly Sita, the heroine of the *Ramayana*. Sita is beautiful, modest, and virtuous in every breath. She is faithful to a husband who nonetheless discards her. In the most popular version of the story, she suffers an unfair fate without complaint—and there is never any question about her chastity. There is no question of her seeking sexual pleasure for her own sake. This vision of the Indian woman that we create is entirely imaginary. And it is her counterpart in the *Mahabharata*— Draupadi—who excites us.

Five husbands! Which straight woman cannot confess to getting a faint thrill while thinking of having five husbands to satisfy her manifold and often conflicting desires?

I imagine that some of the girls I know might want to have five boyfriends. Some of us might fantasize about having sex with a different man each night.

Some of us *want* to have sex each night. I remember Cheryl, who I went to school with, who used to draw explicit pictures of Archie, Betty, and Veronica in the corner of her notebook.

"They're smooching," she would tell me with glee as she flipped the pages to show me. "They're smooching and they like it. And then they're going to have sex for days and days and days. They're going to get married and go on a honeymoon, and have sex for days."

Oh, yes. We want to have sex.

* * *

If Indian girls don't talk about sex, how can we have good sex? Are we even allowed to expect good sex? (After all, we can be dutiful wives and mothers without ever once achieving an orgasm.) Is that something we can be particular about, the way we are expected to be particular over the quality of the dosas we prepare? No, we have other things to worry about than orgasms. For instance, our vaginas, which we must shave and wax and keep tight and white (luckily, there are "intimate washes" that can help us lighten our vaginas until they achieve the ideal shade of whiteness!).

After one unsatisfying encounter, a boy asks me why I don't want to see him any more.

I want to tell him that the sex wasn't good, but I am immediately ashamed of having such a thought. Is mediocre or even bad sex a reason not to have sex with a boy? After all, *he* wants to. And what he wants matters.

One boyfriend—more culturally American than Indian—says, "If you're having your period, you can just go down on me."

I am stunned by the cool impudence of the remark. I restrain the urge to tell him that if cisgender[3] men had periods, we would all be expected to have sex with them even when they were bleeding most heavily. Imagine a world in which their dicks bled once a month. The stigma around period sex would vanish entirely; our mouths would be red from giving them bloody blowjobs.

I want to ask him why he thinks that I don't want to have sex during my period. I wish he would ask me what I want.

But, of course, the cultural script decrees that women do *not* want. It is men who want things. Women are dainty in all their appetites. Who has ever heard of a woman wanting sex as badly as a man?

I think of Mirabai, the Rajput poet renowned for her devotion to Lord Krishna. We speak of her as a great believer, but we delicately skip over the erotic subtext of her poetry. In "I Am Pale with Longing for My Beloved," she writes,

> The sweetness of his lips is a pot of nectar,
> That's the only curd for which I crave

In another poem ("Out in a Downpour"), she says that she is "sopping wet at the doorway" waiting for her Lord. These lines might be read as carnal, but we teach them as spiritual. What does Mirabai want? We do not know because we do not allow space for her wants.

Despite what the historians have said, there is evidence of our wants. There is evidence that we are besharam. Don't forget it.

Men Who Masturbate

I was about nine, I think, when I first saw a man's penis.

We were on the school bus, I distinctly remember. I was not yet sure of what penises were; I had barely any knowledge of my own "down there." I gaped; what was this thing—this dark, swollen bulb that was hanging out of a man's pants?

He was pissing on the street but not with his back to us. He was quite clearly unconcerned about being witnessed. Perhaps, he even preferred it. At any rate, he looked at us with an indescribable expression as we passed, this rickety bus loaded with tiny girls. He didn't break stride in his pissing—the dark yellow jet sloshed down the wall and ran down the pavement.

That encounter is bookended in my own memory with another that came much later, when I was about twenty-seven. I was leaving work, tired and limp in my black suit in July. My car was parked on a side road, one that was not particularly secluded. It was, in fact, right next to a bus stop.

As I waited, shifting my backpack from one shoulder to another, a man caught my attention. His eyes were fixed on me, and he was, I think, mouthing something.

His hands were on his penis and he was rubbing it, up and down, up and down, frantically. I couldn't move.

I think he was trying to come, right there, before my eyes. I finally found my feet and stumbled into my car.

When I compared this to the incident I had witnessed as a child, this one felt worse, much worse. This time, I hadn't seen what his penis looked like, but the vulgarity of that pumping hand felt much worse than anything I could describe. And he hadn't been pissing. No, he had seen me and deliberately taken out his penis so he could masturbate in front of me. In a way, it felt as though this was a sexual encounter that we'd shared. It was as if he had *fucked* me, despite being a good twelve feet away. It was as if I had experienced his penis in a more concrete manner than I actually had. My stunned gaze, my eyes had held his—they had bound us together into a curious kind of intimacy. *Forged.*

* * *

These men who masturbate. Masturbators. These serial offenders.

I spent one summer of my life working for the district attorney's office in Middlesex County, Massachusetts. It was my second year of law school, and I was yet to figure out that I was more inclined to defence than prosecution. So, I made the two-hour journey every morning from Boston, inevitably arriving in a delicate layer of sweat.

In one of the very first cases that I stood up for, I remember the defence requesting a sidebar.

"Your Honor, I would request that the Commonwealth not read the facts."

The Commonwealth—me—was flummoxed.

"Why, Counselor?"

It was a case of a man pulling his penis out near a church. Indecent exposure, they said.

"Because—well, she has an accent. I'd rather she not say the word *scrotum* in front of the court. Makes it sound more salacious."

"X revealed parts of his scrotum to the schoolchildren through the fence."

Was it what I was saying or what he had done? Did an act become less or more salacious while retelling?

Two more cases involving masturbation came up that summer. One was of a man masturbating in a Starbucks outlet. I wasn't working on that case, but I idly skimmed through the files. He'd come in and sat next to a woman eating a blueberry muffin. (Blueberry—my mind clung to that particular detail.) Without warning, he unzipped his pants and began masturbating.

I think I know how close he must have been to her. I triangulated the space from one Starbucks stool to another. Close enough to feel intimate, far enough that you weren't actually touching. Close enough that other people might not see you masturbating.

(One presumes that she dropped the muffin. Or, perhaps, she held on to it. In movies and books, people are always said to be dropping things in times of great agitation. I have found the opposite to be true. When you walk in on your husband in bed with his mistress, you clutch your vase or your coffee cup more tightly.)

The second case was one that we'd heard of in another county. A mistrial that occurred when the jurors went into their private room to deliberate. A man who'd had a crush ("a crush") on another juror held her arm as they were dispersing.

"Just a moment," he told her. "I want to talk to you." She consented to stay behind and at that moment he exposed himself to her. He masturbated. Asked her to touch it. She ran, I think. Naturally. The case was declared a mistrial and the juror was arrested.

Both were unspectacular cases. What they had in common was the audacity displayed. A man touches himself in a public place, a coffee shop, that isn't empty. A man touches himself in a *courtroom*, with policemen outside. The jurors couldn't all have left. They couldn't have been far. Witnesses abound, so why did they do it? Didn't they care that they were being *seen*?

In February 2018, a Delhi University student uploaded a video of a masturbating man on social media. He had been sitting next to her on a bus, touching her waist. Touching himself quietly. Appalled, she began recording the incident on her phone. She shouted at him, but he ignored her completely.

On the video, you can see him ignoring her, continuing to rub his penis. He knows that he is being filmed, but he doesn't care. More astonishingly, you can see that nobody else on the bus seems to care. They ignore her yelling at the man. She would say of the incident later, "People don't even consider something like this as sexual harassment."

I thought of a show I used to watch in college, *The L Word*. It was a bad, soapy show about lipstick lesbians and had overwrought passages of dialogue. *The-Bold-and-the-Beautiful* implausible plotlines. In one scene, a character named Jenny discovers that her male roommate has been spying on her (having installed cameras in her bedroom to catch any instances of lesbian sex). She turns to him and says, with tears in her eyes, "You have a younger sister, don't you? I want you to ask her about the first time she was intruded upon by a man."

He replies, "What makes you think that she was intruded upon?" and Jenny says, "Because there isn't a woman or girl alive in this world who hasn't been intruded upon. And sometimes it is relatively benign. And sometimes it is so fucking painful!"

This is something that we do for ourselves. Without being asked to. We classify the instances in which we are intruded upon. It is a taxonomy of sorts. Some are "relatively benign," and some are "so fucking painful." If a man flashes us in his yard, if a man masturbates in our direction on a crowded bus, are these instances relatively benign?

What would it have taken for the other passengers on the bus to intervene?

* * *

While watching porn one day (my own masturbatory act), I stumble across a particular genre. It is, as far as I can tell, anime and hentai porn, though there are a few live-action videos as well. They are filmed in Japanese subways, on the metro at rush hour. The format is always the same.

A young girl boards a busy train. She is usually wearing a school uniform, including the micro miniskirt of many feverishly masculine imaginations. (Sometimes she is wearing office clothes.) She has no place to sit on the train, so she stands. There is a group of faceless men around her in the dark, their suitcases pressing into the shadows. (Only her face is hyper-visible, each anguished feature on it.) As the train hurtles through the tunnels, one of the men around her takes out his penis.

What happens next varies. Sometimes he rubs it on her; sometimes he rapes her; sometimes he merely masturbates in front of her, holding her gaze the entire time. He may become visible at this point or he may not. Either way, she is visible and trapped. There are hundreds of people around her, but it is unclear whether they are watching. Either they are getting off on it or they are mute.

I am fascinated by this genre of porn. Why does it exist? Clearly, many people are aroused by the thought of a man publicly masturbating on a woman.

I try and look for the same scenario, gender-flipped. There are none.

masturbatory (comparative more *masturbatory*, superlative most *masturbatory*): Of or relating to masturbation. Excessively self-absorbed or self-indulgent.[1]

"Excessive self-indulgence" is something Indian men know well. I was alarmed when I moved back to India and found how much men insisted on talking. Not that talking is the exclusive domain of the *Indian* male (Dale Spender has extensively documented— and debunked—the perception that women talk more than men!). But, certainly, Indian men seem to talk without having much to say. Men like Arnab Goswami speak so loudly on panels that they might as well be shouting.

The lectures. There's always one man after the lecture (*always* a man) who asks a question designed exclusively to show off his intelligence and to flatter the lecturer (if he is male).

"Sir, I had some thoughts . . ."

Sometimes, if there is a moderator, they try to avoid this behavior. "Is this a question?"

"Yes," says the man confidently.

It is never a question. This man merely wants to deliver his own mini lecture. It reminds me of college classes in which we were rewarded for commenting on the lecture. For these men, the sound of their own voice is rewarding enough.

They are on panels too. Always running over time, always finding so much more to say, because what they have to say is so important. When women like Barkha Dutt speak with an ounce of their confidence, they are described as harsh, shrill, feminazi termagants. Always interrupting me at work, confidently explaining why they are right and I am wrong, or why I don't know enough. Always pulling me aside to tell me what they have to say.

"Listen, *beta*," says an old man, confidently drinking his Black Label on the rocks. (It is always Black Label on the rocks.) He proceeds to tell me a long, boring, and irrelevant story about his work, or his hobbies, or the British empire. It doesn't seem to matter that I'm not interested. He never asks me if I'm interested (and never considers that the British empire is almost certainly irrelevant to my life). There are so many old men like him, and so many middle-aged men too, who have a captive audience in the young. Particularly young women to whom they can hold forth. Pontificate. *Masturbate.*

"Witness me," shout the group titled "War Boys" in a movie I'm watching that summer (a movie that incidentally angered men for being "too feminist"). The phrase sticks in my head. A cry to people watching. See me. Look at me. You *will* witness me.

That's what these men do. Chronic masturbators like Louis C.K., whom so many women have accused of sexual misconduct. When the comedy duo Dana Min Goodman and Julia Wolov met C.K. in his hotel room, he asked if he could "take out his penis." They said that they thought he was joking. But then he stripped naked and masturbated,[2] while the women sat "paralyzed." A man like C.K., a man who could no doubt enlist any number of women who were willing to watch him masturbate, who would have provided actual consent to the act? But he didn't go down the consensual route.[3]

When the story broke, several men came forward to say that Goodman and Wolov had consented. *Why didn't they leave?* asked the men angrily. Confused. *How could you be paralyzed?* I think about what I would have done in a similar situation, if I were faced with a man I idolized masturbating in front of me. Surely, I would have nervously laughed too. I would have thought "ohgodthisishappeningwhyisthishappening" as C.K. took it out and masturbated.

I would have been paralyzed too.

* * *

Even when they *don't* masturbate, we are witnesses.

When men give up masturbation, they write articles about it. They make movies out of it. I type "I gave up masturbating" into Google, and it returns more than three million results. I only need to scan the first few pages to see that almost all the people talking about giving up masturbation are men. They talk about how it has changed their lives, what physical fulfillment and spiritual clarity they have attained after not masturbating for thirty, sixty, 100 days.

Where are the women? Where are the women who masturbate?

There is almost no proof that Indian women masturbate, beside the odd, suspiciously shaped massager that is sold in international airports. For one thing, where is the time? For another, where is the *space*? The vast majority of Indian women do not have an ounce of privacy. From the moment they wake up to the moment they sleep next to their husbands, they are barely alone. There is always someone—the dhobi, the lauki-seller, or the neighbor who has come to exchange mail or gossip. The hovering mother-in-law. No privacy.

And still, I am convinced, Indian women are masturbating. Indian women who are so good at living in interstitial spaces. They lock themselves in bathrooms, just for a moment. Perhaps, when they've got the baby to sleep or when no one can hear them, under the covers at night. Without vibrators, without porn, without sex toys or lube. They pleasure themselves because no one else will. They masturbate because they are human beings and all human beings masturbate. Even though we are told that only men do.

Perhaps, it is the punishment of cis women. After all, it is our biology. The vagina is inward. Retreating. A vagina is a not a weapon. It would be difficult for women to squat on the road and thrust our vaginas obscenely at anyone. We cannot point our quivering vaginas *at* anyone when we masturbate.

I often think about how vaginas are shaped. How even in Georgia O'Keeffe's flamboyant renderings of vaginas, they look discreet, tucked away. There is a neatness to the female form, I think, as I regard Gustave Courbet's 1866 painting *The Origin of the World*. In the painting, a naked woman's body lies sprawled in front of the viewer. However, even in this frank state, there is a certain mystery about it. A thick thatch of hair hides the clitoris. From this point of view, I imagine a penis would look . . . less majestic than comic.

Is that part of God's design too? After all, serial masturbators are mocked. I think of this when I receive a WhatsApp video of a man jacking off while saying my name. "You did this," he whispers, pointing to his swollen and monstrous penis. (A favorite saying of men, I think. Despite the incontrovertible fact that I have done nothing.)

I have not asked for this video. He has sent it to me without warning, without my consent. I watch it unmoved. It is not offensive so much as pathetic. Who wants to watch a man jacking off? I cannot find any porn videos that feature a man jacking off alone. (A woman touching herself, on the contrary, is highly marketable and such videos are numerous.)

I read a sentence in some review of a mediocre book of poetry: "The loneliness of the flasher, who has no one to talk to. A penis is a smoke signal begging to be noticed." It is a man, of course, who is saying this about another man's poem. (Continuing the grand tradition of men forgiving men. Always reminding us where to direct the jet of our empathy.)

The flasher is lonely. The penis is ridiculous. C.K. is a sad man, who should be pitied. If we laugh, how can we condemn? After all, these are lonely men. No one will witness them, and men *deserve* to be witnessed.

What is funny cannot be violent.

On Holi, they tell us not to go outside. Apparently, men in Delhi are flinging balloons filled with cum at women.

When I read this news, I cannot find words to describe the tightening in my chest. I think of the vileness of this, the grotesqueness of a balloon of cum exploding on a woman. It is the act of masturbation stretched to its final, logical endpoint. The money shot in porn.

After all, as long as we don't have to see it, it is fine, right? Even if we see it, it's fine. As long as it didn't get on us. At least it didn't get in us or make us pregnant. See? We're actually lucky. It's masturbation, not rape. *Sometimes the trespass is relatively benign.* "People don't consider something like this as sexual harassment."

I'm saying enough is enough! I'm saying I'm tired. I cannot stomach these men any more. I do not want to see their vile penises. I do not want to see them masturbate in every arena of public life. Men jacking off is not new to me nor is it important. If I am seeing it without my consent, that is a *crime.* No less important than any other crime. Sometimes, I long to reach within me, pluck out the youngest version of myself—who had not yet known the hierarchy of male trespasses—and remind her. There are things she is not expected to witness. There are things nobody should tolerate.

Uncomfortable Women

What are we teaching our men and boys about female sex and pleasure?

In December 2017, the *New Yorker* published a short piece by Kristen Roupenian. It was called "Cat Person," and it detailed an unsavory sexual encounter between a twenty-year-old college girl named Margot and an older man. Almost as soon as it was published, it went viral: it became one of the most read pieces of 2017. Women everywhere were sharing it with the commentary "this happened to me!" or "this is all too real." Other women were surprised by the ubiquity of the experience: nothing like that had happened to *them*. However, the virality of the piece (its author eventually secured a seven-figure book deal) meant that it had tapped into a female vein. Evidently, it had managed to say something about the straight female experience. In particular, the *uncomfortable* female experience.

Tutorial #1: Physical Pressure

Listen, I want to tell you about one night in my life. It was only one night, and it happened a long time ago. I have had other nights like it. It is the kind of night that is frighteningly commonplace for women.

It is winter in Delhi, the kind of winter that is foggy and bracingly cold but not unbearable. On an impulse, I decide to call a boy over. It is late at night—1 A.M., or maybe 2 A.M.—and I'm drunk on cheap whiskey, the kind that only costs 200 rupees per bottle. The boy I'm texting is a stopgap. I don't really like him, but I'm heartbroken and I know he likes me (or, at least, he wants me). He looked me over in a dim basement where I was dressed as Lara Croft—for a Halloween party—and asked a mutual friend to introduce us.

The attention feels good. (Or, at least, it feels like something.) It feels like a promise that life will go on, that there will be boys beside the one that broke my heart. When he asks me if we can hang out, I give him my address. Then I drink the rest of the Kingfisher I'm holding and sprint upstairs to make sure my breath smells fresh.

As it turns out, I need not have bothered. We are standing on my terrace, overlooking the quiet road when he starts kissing me. His breath is rank in my mouth and he is a terrible kisser: he mashes his mouth over mine in a frankly hideous way. But what does it matter? I steer him gently to the bedroom, wanting this to be over quickly.

Slices. I am drunk enough to remember it in slices. There is not much more kissing. He pulls my pants down and bites the soft flesh of my thighs. I don't understand—how can he think this is pleasurable? I'll have large bruises the next day. I flinch and squirm, which he mistakes for excitement. It only animates him more, and though we cannot have penetrative sex (he is far too drunk for that), he wriggles on top of me some more ineptly before we both mercifully fall asleep.

It is 9 A.M. when I wake up feeling groggy. This is well before I usually wake up, and I'm confused till I understand that the boy in my bed is on top of me. He's trying to kiss my neck again, to wake me up.

I'm not drunk any more, but I don't feel well. I'm hungover and I don't want to have sex. I push him off (ungently). But he keeps coming back, groping my breasts urgently. He takes his shirt and trousers off and thrusts his flaccid dick into my unwilling mouth.

At that moment, I wonder what we look like from above. I was raised on Hollywood-style sex scenes, on vignettes of hands grasping silken sheets. I have seen what loving, consensual, *sexy* sex looks like. In those moments, it is clear that the women are enjoying themselves. They sigh and moan and their toes curl. They reach out a hand to the headboard and push their hips urgently against their partners'.

None of what is happening now looks like that. There is nothing sexy about this. It is not violent, no. It doesn't look like those films that pass Bollywood censors. There is no screaming, no crying. I'm not fighting him. I'm not saying "no."

What is happening is that he is pushing a woman to do something that she is uncomfortable with, even if it is not penetrative sex or "rape." Instead of coming forward, I'm going back. I'm squirming away. I'm pushing his heavy body off mine, but he doesn't stop. He unzips his pants and puts a hand on the back of my head until I am choking on his cock.

It's not assault. But it is something that shouldn't be happening. He shouldn't be trying to have sex with a woman who isn't interested. I think that much is fair to say. To expect.

The best way I can think of to describe it is that he is seeing my resistance as immaterial. I find this with some men—they think of you as a goalpost. How do I get in? Anything that keeps me from getting in, I will overcome. Of course, women aren't going to be enthusiastic about this. *Of course*, they will sigh, turn over, say "not now" or "I don't want to do this." It is their collective chant to each other. *Keep pushing, bro! Keep pushing!*

Eventually—not before he bites the insides of my thighs some more—I excuse myself, saying I have to go to the loo. Once there, I splash some water on my hot face. I say I have to make a phone call and on this pretext, I lock myself in another room.

He knocks. He rings my phone. I wait. After waiting for me to return for half an hour (*keep pushing, bro!*), he leaves.

I wonder what he thought about where I was. Why I did not come out of my room. I wonder what he thought about during the sex. It could not have been very good for him, could it? Having sex with a woman who is clearly resistant to the idea?

"She's trash in bed, bro. Just lay there the whole time and stared at the ceiling. Frigid bitch."

How many of the women they describe as bad in bed are women like me? Unhappy women? Women who are passive during an unpleasant encounter? How many of them are women who just give in because it is easier to give in rather than shout or scream?

Trembling, I get back into bed. I lie curled up, my back to the wall. I examine my thighs. As I thought, he has created blossoming purple bruises that will soon turn yellow and green. I hug myself, trying to be tender with a body that has not been treated very tenderly. I stay like that for a long time.

* * *

In law school, we took a class on ethics. It was one of the most interesting classes offered; we spent our days wrestling with the trolley problem[1] and whether it was ethical to torture prisoners for information (instead of debating knotty points of contract law). I loved the class for forcing me to confront so many of the assumptions and stereotypes that had built up and ossified in my mind. There were no real rules or answers. Just as with the trolley problem. Well, maybe it is okay to torture a prisoner if doing so would help you save ten children. What if you only tortured him a little? Wouldn't that be a fair exchange? We tossed around *yes* and *no* and *it depends* with ease, but the professor refused to give us neat solutions or confirm that anything we were saying was correct.

One day when I walked into class, I found a handout on my desk. "Yes Means Yes: The New Consent Model for Feminism." After quickly skimming it, I made some notes. Apparently, it referred to a theory of consent that feminists were pushing. (At the time, I did not identify as a feminist.) They were saying that it was not enough to use the "no" model. According to them, sex between two partners required enthusiastic consent from both parties. More than that, each sexual act required enthusiastic consent.

I tried to imagine it. It seemed a little funny to me. A little mechanical, surely? In practice?

"May I go down on you now?"

"Yes."

"Now, may I put my penis inside you?"

"Yes."

I smirked. Just then, a boy on the other side of the room raised his hand.

It was E, who was well known in law school for his rigidly conservative views. Boston was a liberal city and most of the people I knew were cheerfully progressive. However, I was pretty sure that E was a member of the Federalist Society (which was composed entirely of men who would go on to become Republican senators).[2] He was most certainly *not* a feminist.

"Don't you think this would kill romance? I mean, this sounds so awful. So, it's not enough to ask permission before you kiss a girl? Do you need to stop every thirty seconds while you're having sex with her? To ask permission? What happened to romance?"

Despite the fact that I had been thinking something along the same lines, I turned and stared at him in outrage. E had some nerve putting the question in that way—nobody who looked at him could conclude he was deeply concerned about romance. I'd never seen him with a woman and I couldn't believe that a boy with such a sickly pallor and Henry-the-VIIIth inbred face could be very sexually active.

No, he wasn't concerned about dating or romance. He was merely putting the question that any men's rights activist would put to the professor. *Don't you think feminism is going too far?*

Without even thinking about it, I raised my hand. It was one of those classes where the professor preferred to be minimally involved and so he had us battle each other directly.

"Well, considering the alternative is non-consensual sex, I think that the solution they propose is worth it. Even if people have to ask for permission every thirty seconds, it's worth it."

He looked at me carefully, patiently, as if he were dealing with an idiot whom he had to instruct slowly.

"That is a false framing of the problem," he said with conviction. "This model is unnecessary. If these women are about to have sex that they do not want to have, they can just say *no*. There was nothing wrong with the old no model."

"Oh, can they?" My blood was up now. "And it's *just that easy*, is it? What about nonverbal nos?"

E scoffed. "No such thing. Let me ask you this: how are men supposed to understand nonverbal nos? Are we mind readers? Which miraculous gesture is a clear nonverbal no?"

I was upset now. I was well and truly upset. So much so that the professor was watching me with worry. I didn't know this at the time, but I had been, what a psychologist would call, *triggered*.[3]

"There is!" I spluttered. "There are certain physical responses—freezing up or pushing the man away—that your body has to danger. At that moment, it might be difficult to say *no*. But that doesn't mean you're consenting. There are clear signals of nonverbal nos. And also of nonverbal consent. If a woman is enthusiastic about something, you can tell! It's the difference between kissing someone and being kissed back."

He crossed his arms and looked away. I could tell I'd lost him.

"It sets a dangerous precedent. People can speak up if they don't want something."

I could feel the tears coming. It is the most common way my body betrays me, to show emotion when I'm furious.

"May I be excused?" I asked the professor. When he nodded yes, I bolted to the bathroom and cried. Hot, messy tears. I was angry, but I was shaking too. I couldn't explain why, other than the feeling that he had been blaming me. I felt that he had been accusing me. *Priya, you should have said something. If you were uncomfortable, you should have said so. Are you so weak that you can't say no?*

No.

I think of the time when a man—my boss—wrapped his hand around my waist at an office party. It was late—maybe 1 A.M.—and we had all been drinking heavily. We were standing close together and it was a friendly office. (In retrospect, too friendly.)[4] He did it very casually and he left his hand there. It wasn't a grope. It was just his arm around my waist. Like I was a rail that he could hold on to steady himself on the subway.

I felt it was odd. If I were in his position—he was older, married, and *my boss*—I would have cut off my arm before doing that to a colleague. Surely he knew the impropriety of it?

I hesitated, looking around the room. Everybody seemed perfectly unconcerned. None of them were saying anything or even looking at my boss. Perhaps, this was normal? In any case, I felt I could not say anything. Everybody was having such a good time. What right did I have to spoil it? If I felt uncomfortable, that was *my* problem to deal with. Wasn't it?

It is this that echoes in my mind when I hear a boy at a party say, "Man, why do you have to make a fuss?" He is saying it to a girl who has accused another partygoer of touching her inappropriately. I almost see it from his point of view. The girl has gone to the hosts. She's making a scene, yelling and cussing at the groper. Now the music has been paused and everybody is trying to sort out the mess. Wouldn't it have been easier if she hadn't said anything?

Our discomfort is the price we are willing to pay for buying men's happiness.

It is a conversation I have seen in real life too many times. A girl not able to muster enough courage to call out bad or inappropriate behavior. Say, a boy has said something sexual to her that she didn't appreciate and now feels uncomfortable. She brings it up hesitantly. Couches it in the least offensive way possible. The gentlest and the least hostile manner.

"Hey, man. I thought what you did—that comment you made about my body—wasn't cool. It made me feel weird."

The boy can react in two ways: either by being overly aggressive or denying it entirely.

"What? No way! You're just being sensitive. That wasn't what I meant at *all*."

Or—and this is worse—he can be sensitive and feel *bad* about it.

"Oh, wow. I'm so sorry. I feel so terrible that I made you feel uncomfortable. Really. I never do that. I'm not that type of guy."

He goes on and on, mired in shame and shock. Finally, the girl provides a mitigating statement.

"Don't worry about it. I mean, it's not a big deal. I just thought I'd let you know that I felt weird."

"No, seriously. I feel terrible! That's not like me at all. I'm usually great at reading the room, you know? I really try to respect women in everything that I do and be considerate. I mean, that's what my mother taught me, you know? Those are my principles. Fuck. I feel so shitty!"

The girl sighs.

"Yeah. I can understand. Look, it's fine. You seem like a great guy. Let's put the whole thing behind us now."

What's happened? Now the girl is being forced to console the boy. To prop up his temporarily injured ego. To minimize her own discomfort, because *he* feels uncomfortable. After all, he's apologized. What more does she want? Why can't she let it go? One thing she can be sure of is that he will keep pushing her until she does. God forbid he sits for a while in the knowledge of his wrongness. God forbid he feels bad about himself for longer than two minutes.

A man feeling bad is not the same as an apology. An apology is not the same as changed behavior (the man in my hypothetical situation is only a while away from offending her again). And an apology does not require acceptance. These are things we do not teach our women and girls. Why? Why do we only teach our men to keep pushing?

Why do they not leave when they make girls uncomfortable? Why do they not simply *stop?*

Tutorial #2: Badgering

On spring break a couple of years ago, my long-distance boyfriend at the time, A, broke up with me. He called me on a Friday night to "talk about our relationship." I did not understand what that was code for but I knew it had to be serious.

It was the worst possible time to call me. I was at a friend's apartment, which was filled with loud drunk people. (She had a habit of collecting people at the bar—anybody and everybody she could find at 2 A.M. to make her loneliness seem less lonely.) There were black boys and white girls and drug dealers from Southie (South Boston) littered throughout her huge, expensive apartment.

I went to her bedroom to talk to A in privacy. She was about to graduate and move out, and I remember the room had been emptied. Since there was nothing to sit on, I sat on the floor with my back to the wall.

There wasn't much to say. I had known it was coming for some time, if I'm telling the truth. There was something about the flavor of our last conversations; a chill when I had kissed him goodbye and headed to the airport. I had gone through his Facebook pictures looking for other women and I had analyzed the angle at which his hand rested on their hips. I knew it was over because I was thinking of the first conversation we had had about being Indians in America. What was it Junot Diaz had once said? "As soon as you start thinking about the beginning, it's the end."

I wasn't in love with him, but I didn't want the relationship to end. It felt humiliating that he could so quickly and cleanly sever his ties with me. Even if he couldn't, that's what it seemed like.

It was an intense conversation, which quickly denigrated into drunken sobbing at my end. He sounded ashamed.

"It's not working for me. Maybe, in the future, if we lived in the same city, we could pick things up again," he said nicely. A punch wrapped in a soft scarf. I only sobbed harder.

Then I saw the bedroom door open. I didn't know what was happening—perhaps, my friend had come in because she was concerned? I was about to tell her that I would talk to her later, but then I saw it was one of the guys from the party. To my amazement, he walked into the dark room and sat next to me, crossing his legs, as if he was just getting comfortable.

It wasn't as though I had been weeping silently. I had been sobbing loudly. You could not mistake what I was doing.

I said to my boyfriend—now my ex-boyfriend—*hang on*. My surprise had overcome my hurt at that moment.

"What's going on? What are you doing here?"

He said, "No, I just want to hang out with you. It's fine, continue with your call. I'll be quiet."

Obediently, I picked up the phone again. I could not make sense of what he wanted, but perhaps he was trying to comfort me? This large man whom I did not know. Perhaps, he was trying to make me feel better by providing me company?

The call went on for a good twenty minutes after that. I didn't care that the strange man was sitting next to me; I abandoned myself to the excesses of grief. Despite my intoxication, I understood that this was not a negotiable breakup. I would not be able to change my mind. When A did anything, he committed to it fully. He simply didn't want me any more.

When we finally hung up, I was even more upset than before. There was mascara running down my face; my nice outfit had crumpled and was reeking of vodka where someone had spilled their drink on it. It was very late, around 4 A.M., and everybody must have left, as the house was quiet. Good. I could cry myself to sleep in peace.

I'd forgotten about the man sitting next to me, but then he put a hand on my leg and said, "I think you did the right thing there."

He must have sensed my incredulity because he explained, "I'm sorry about that, but all the points you made, I think you were right about them. It's best to just end a relationship like that. If it's long distance and you're unhappy, I mean."

I said, "Sorry, who ARE you? Why are you here? Why aren't you in the living room? Where . . . who did you come with?"

He wouldn't give me a straight answer. He mumbled something about there being no party left, about his friend having gone to hook up with mine.

"I wanted to give them some time together."

I got up and checked; he was telling the truth. Nobody was in the living room.

I rattled my friend's bedroom doorknob gently, but there was no answer—she'd locked it. Perhaps, she was having sex with one of the strays she'd picked up at the bar. Perhaps, she was asleep. I returned to the living room and put a cushion and blanket on the floor. I'd sleep here. I didn't care.

"I think you should leave now," I said to the man who hovered in the doorway, watching me. "As you can see, there's obviously no party left."

"I want to stay," he said, coming over and patting my leg through the blanket. "I can stay and cuddle with you and make you feel better."

I stared in amazement. "I don't want to cuddle with anyone. I just broke up with my boyfriend! I don't want to touch anyone." I had never been so blunt with a man but grief made my words direct and plain.

"But I—"

And I knew this was the beginning again, the start of a long, wearisome cycle of badgering. He would wear me down until I assented softly to being cuddled and then he would slip his hand under my shirt and begin touching me in various places. Calculating how he would fuck me. When he would get to fuck me. Whatever nos I issued—direct or indirect—he would see them as the beginning of a negotiation. He would not go away until he had fucked me.

I was so tired that I contemplated telling him "okay." I could lie down and open my legs for him. Wouldn't that just be easier for all of us? If I cut to the chase? I was so tired.

I told him no. As I thought, he stayed and tried for an hour. When he finally left, putting his hat on, shambling his way to the door, filled with confusion and frustration, I wondered if he knew how close I had come to giving in.

Of course, he knew. That was why he did it. He didn't care that I was sad. It was easier for him because I was sad. In him, I saw (fairly or unfairly) a thousand other boys. The ones who scanned dimly lit bars, searching always for the sad girl on the barstool. "Are you feeling vulnerable?" *Vulnerable enough to fuck me?*

I cannot understand it. What is it in these men that makes them want to persuade women, to badger them until they give in? I think of all the times I have had to escort men personally to the door. Even good men. Even friends of mine.[5] They always sat there long past their welcome, trying to touch my foot or hand or any part that they could. To begin the manipulation and the debate.

I just want to cuddle you.
I just want to make you feel good.
I just want to go down on you. We don't have to fuck.
I just want to help you feel better.
It'll be so good.
I promise.

When men tell me that saying no is easy, I wonder how many times they have badgered women themselves. I wonder how many soft nos they have bludgeoned past and pretended they did not notice. I wonder who teaches them this. Because, surely, it must be hard on the ego to sleep with people who do not want to sleep with you. I have never slept with anybody who wasn't excited to sleep with me, who did not want me badly. Where and how do men learn this: the art of badgering? They would not badger other men. (If they did, the matter would be settled with fists.)

I read a #MeToo article on Aziz Ansari.[6] It describes an encounter he had with a young girl called Grace (name changed to protect her identity). The Internet blows up over this article. Everywhere, men are angry, telling us Ansari should not be lumped with Harvey Weinstein (they have only recently, reluctantly, accepted that Weinstein is a rapist, and only after the incontrovertible proofs offered by multiple women). After all, they say, this Ansari story is only of a date gone bad.

Here are some select passages from Grace's account of the events. The full version was originally posted online on Babe.[7] These parts are the moments in which Grace felt uncomfortable and expressed verbal and nonverbal cues of disinterest.

When Ansari told her he was going to grab a condom within minutes of their first kiss, Grace voiced her *hesitation* explicitly. "I said something like, '*Whoa, let's relax for a sec, let's chill*.'" She says he then resumed kissing her, briefly performed oral sex on her and asked her to do the same thing to him [. . .]

Ansari also physically pulled her hand towards his penis multiple times throughout the night, from the time he first kissed her on the countertop. "He probably moved my hand to his dick five to seven times," she said. "He really kept doing it after I *moved it away*."

But the main thing was that *he wouldn't let her move away from him* [. . .]

Throughout the course of her short time in the apartment, she says she used verbal and non-verbal cues to indicate how uncomfortable and distressed she was. "*Most of my discomfort was expressed in me pulling away and mumbling. I know that my hand stopped moving at some points*," she said. "*I stopped moving my lips and turned cold.*

[. . .] "But he kept asking, so I said, '*Next time.*'

[. . .] "I said *I don't want to feel forced* because then I'll hate you, and I'd rather not hate you," she said.

"After he bent me over is *when I stood up and said no, I don't think I'm ready to do this, I really don't think I'm going to do this* [. . .]"

While the TV played in the background, he kissed her again, stuck his fingers down her throat again and moved to undo her pants. *She turned away* [. . .]

After that last kiss, Grace *stood up from the couch, moved back to the kitchen island where she left her phone and said she would call herself a car.* [Emphasis added.]

There's a lot going on here. When men read this, they may note that Grace did, in fact, go down on Ansari. They may point to that as proof that she consented to everything that took place (of course, this is an erroneous view of consent).

Yes, she did go down on Ansari briefly. But I think it's important to keep in mind the power dynamics at work here: Grace is twenty-two. Ansari is over a decade older. She is a nobody, a photographer. She is in the apartment of a famous man, an older man, a man she has likely idolized up to that point. (There must have been some natural shock that a man who built a reputation on being nice to women was not being nice to her.) There are countless pressures bearing down on Grace. Put all this in context and ask yourself: how free would you have felt? How easy would it have been for *you* to resist? As a hesitant twenty-two-year-old girl?

Let's look at the times she *did* resist. Pulling away countless times. So many times. So many nonverbal expressions of disinterest. Freezing, mumbling, closing her mouth, standing up from the couch, shaking him off at almost every touch, at every point. One would have to be blind or lack the sensation of touch to be ignorant of Grace's disinterest.

Okay, fine. Ignore anything nonverbal. Let's turn our attention to what's been said. From the transcript of the conversation, I count four verbal expressions of disinterest. Four! They range from the mild "whoa, let's relax, let's chill" to the outright alarming "I don't want to feel forced because then I'll hate you."

I don't want to feel forced?

What is forced sex?

Rape.

This statement should have instantly set off red flags in any man's head. But, remember, we are not just dealing with any man. This is no clueless Philistine. We are talking about Aziz motherfuckin' Ansari, the thirty-five-year-old man who literally wrote a book on dating called *Modern Romance*. Ansari is not an unseasoned, unaware man. He has made a tremendous amount of money based on his reputation as a feminist. (Even in that interaction with Grace he brings it up: "It's only fun if we're both having fun." Almost immediately, he contradicts his words.)

One of his most famous routines from his stand-up specials is about dick pics. It's quite something. He stands in front of an enormous audience and shouts exuberantly: "Ladies get unsolicited dick pics! All the *time*. Isn't that crazy? That's so crazy! Men are out here sending women pictures of their dicks! Wow! Why would you *do* that?"[8] [Emphasis added.]

Not only does he do "feminist stand-up," but he has also written, starred in, and produced two seasons of the hit TV show *Master of None*. In an early episode of the show, a woman is frightened because a man is following her home from the bar. The man follows her for blocks because he cannot sense her discomfort. Or, more pertinently, *he does not care*.

It is a short scene—it only lasts about five minutes in a whole episode on feminism—but is astonishingly well written. As this nervous young woman looks over her shoulder, takes well-lit roads that are longer, avoids shortcuts, we see intercut scenes of Ansari walking home with a friend. They are walking gaily, with nonchalance, because they are men. (It is gaiety that speaks words about the invisible costs of womanhood.) Overall, the scene is poignant, haunting.

And this is from the brain of the man who gave a young woman the worst night of her life because he would not stop forcing himself on her!

Men are afraid, they say, in this era of #MeToo. They talk about feeling victimized (a flipping of the truth that is so deft I almost admire it). They are scared now, they protest. They write op-eds in newspapers about "not knowing how to behave now." Millennial women have killed dating. They wring their hands over "not being able to harmlessly compliment women at work now." (How many of these men are harmless complimenters and how many are men like R.K. Pachauri?) They wince at the flood of Facebook posts on their timeline from women. They draw back and complain. Above all, they say one thing: "Not me. I am not guilty. I did not know. How could I have known? I would rather die than make a woman uncomfortable," they claim. "If I had only known that she was uncomfortable, surely, I would have done something."

To that, I have nothing to say but no. I reject the notion that men do not understand what is happening when women are uncomfortable. I reject it out of hand. I do not believe them when they say that complimenting their secretary's legs was innocent. I do not believe them when they say that the strings of text messages and unanswered phone calls were kindly meant. I do not believe them when they plead ignorance of the fact that we are in pain, that we are uncomfortable, that we *do not want this*. No. I do not think that custom or a motive of affection excuses the creepy Indian uncles who let their hands linger so long around our waists while we try to wriggle out of their grip. I do not buy their story that they weren't cognizant of our anxiety and fear. I do not believe that there are any circumstances in which it is okay to keep pushing, to keep badgering and breaking down and forcing yourself on a person who is not happy. Whose face and body language and gestures are screaming, "No!" *No*. Even when she does not say no.

No, the word which is so hard for Indian women to pronounce. For so long we have been gracious; for so long we have been told that our discomfort does not matter. Anyway, how comfortable have we ever been? Can we imagine a world in which we can be comfortable all the time? When have we had it?

But now let me tell you a happy story.

It is a late night at a bar—I'm with my girlfriend and she is giggling deliciously with me about a "dick I might like to try." (She is as shameless as I am.) This is something that we do quite often—we make a list of men who have good dicks and share them with each other. In this era of men watching too much porn and being plagued by whiskey dick, a man who can dick you down properly is an absolute gift from God.

I look at the man she's describing. He's not my usual type but I can't forget her words. Sometimes, you just need to be dicked down properly.

Later, when we're at my house decompressing from the night, he asks me if he should leave. He's the last one; my friends have all gone.

He says it in the *chill*-est possible fashion. "I can leave if you want." Like, *of course*, he would leave if I didn't want to do anything.

I'm amazed by the kindness of this gesture. At least there is time for me to think about what I want—if I want him to stay or leave. I realize that this is a choice that has been made for me many times.

"You don't have to leave if you don't want to."

We lie down on my bed, elbows barely touching.

Before he kisses me, he asks for permission. I appreciate the way he has phrased it. It's the subtlest way to ask for permission. When he does kiss me, it is good. Slow. He takes everything a little more slowly than other men—waiting for me to take off my own top before he undresses.

He pauses with a hand on my hair. *How do you feel about your hair being pulled?* His hand hovers over my ass before he spanks me. *How do you feel about being spanked?* When he asks me these questions, it does not take me out of the moment. I am still right there with him, feeling turned on. No romance has been lost. He has merely asked me for my consent. It is so strange that he understands this: *consent is ongoing.* That one cannot bully and badger a girl into sex and then take that as blanket permission to do with her body what you will.

Afterwards, I feel relaxed. I have no shame or guilt or self-loathing. It occurs to me that this is how men must usually feel after sex. It is not such a common feeling for me.

This is the world that I want to make for women. *This.* I want nothing more than for us to feel comfortable, to be free of men pushing and badgering. For our boundaries to be respected. It is such a simple thing that I want to cry. That is all we ask.

II
UGLINESS

Beauty

"I had only one desire: to dismember it. To see of what it was made, to discover the dearness, to find the beauty, the desirability that had escaped me, but apparently only me."
—Toni Morrison, *The Bluest Eye*

I

When I was a little girl, my mother bought a doll for me. It was from an expensive boutique in Paris. She had rosy cheeks and long dreamy lashes. Her eyes were blue and they closed when you lay her down. When you propped her up, they opened. I was fascinated by how lifelike this attribute was, but what amazed me the most, were the colors of her eyes and her skin: so blue! so white! I named her Sleeping Beauty.

Sleeping Beauty's real name has always varied: some call her Briar Rose, some call her Rosamond. Disney calls her Aurora. However, in the most popular version of the story, Charles Perrault left the princess anonymous. Before falling into a deep sleep, she is called Beauty, because she has been given the gift of perfect beauty by her fairy godmother. While she sleeps, she is called Sleeping Beauty, for that is all she is. When the prince comes to rescue her, he finds her in her beautiful bedchamber, sleeping. Fixed; passive; perfectly beautiful. He falls in love with her beauty, what else does he know of her?

The brown/black is only coded as beautiful when it retains a certain percentage of whiteness. It's a phenomenon that works both ways. In reverse, it's what I call *featural appropriation*. The features that are mocked or satirized on the black/brown body are praised when transplanted on to a white woman. Like cultural appropriation, it is a systematic deconstruction of our culture, our features. Some of our parts are taken and the rest are discarded on the floor. We are discarded.

II

Jasmine's precursor is, of course, Princess Badroulbadour from *One Thousand and One Nights*. She is described as

> The most beautiful brunette in the world; her eyes were large, lively, and sparkling; her looks sweet and modest; her nose was of a just proportion and without a fault; her mouth small, her lips of a vermilion red, and charmingly agreeable symmetry; in a word, all the features of her face were perfectly regular.[1]

Compare this description to Jules Verne's in *Around the World in Eighty Days*:

> [. . .] Her fine eyes resumed all their soft Indian expression. When the poet-king, Ucaf Uddaul, celebrates the charms of the queen of Ahmehnagara, he speaks thus: "Her shining tresses, divided in two parts, encircle the harmonious contour of her white and delicate cheeks, brilliant in their glow and

freshness. Her ebony brows have the form and charm of the bow of Kama, the god of love, and beneath her long silken lashes the purest reflections and a celestial light swim, as in the sacred lakes of Himalaya, in the black pupils of her great clear eyes."[2]

Princess Badroulbadour is described as having "perfectly regular" features, because regularity and symmetry are pleasing to the eye; they are charming, agreeable, faultless. If beauty is described as regular and faultless, we presume that ugliness is the opposite. Something irregular, some fundamental fault line in the topography of the female face, some fearful *a*symmetry that causes ugliness. Ucaf Uddaul describes the queen's charms similarly: her cheeks have "harmonious contours." What is ugly is not merely ugly then. It offends harmony. It offends symmetry.

Verne goes on to describe Aouda as a "charming woman in all the European acceptation of the phrase." Her eyes have a "soft Indian expression." She is described as fundamentally an Other but still acceptable by European standards of beauty, which is paramount. Verne, in his benevolence, makes sure to let us know that the particular kind of foreign beauty that Aouda has does not prevent her from fitting into the mold that would be considered a beautiful woman in England.

I had an Indian friend once ask me on a trip home: "What do white boys think of Indian women? Do they think we're pretty?" The question hurt me, just as it hurt me to see a YouTube comment on a Selena Gomez song called "Come and Get It," where she crooned over an old Indian song, "I'm Indian and proud to see that Selena Gomez likes our culture. I never thought people would know so much about India like she does [sic]." (In live performances of the song, she is wearing a bindi.)

Both were shaded with such innocence that how could I possibly begin to explain to either person the complex realities surrounding their assumptions? More importantly, I thought, I didn't need to. Perhaps it would be enough to just say, "White people's opinion of our beauty, our culture, doesn't matter." But then, who would be satisfied with that answer? How can I describe the specific wound left on online dating sites by white women who say "only white men" or that left by white men who say "you're attractive, for an (X ethnicity)?" We do not dare disclaim or minimize the woundedness of little brown girls. We know what happens to a wound when it festers.

III

Beauty is pain, goes the saying, but what does it mean? My grandmother tells me it means that one must suffer to be beautiful. There is a certain kind of suffering, perhaps, in female beauty rituals. We pluck our eyebrows, wax our legs, ache in our stilettos. We go hungry and zip ourselves into dresses that make it difficult to walk. And still, I am dissatisfied with the construction of that phrase. Is it instead, pain is beautiful?

Many men have told me they are attracted to sad girls, who are in pain and need to be rescued. There is a romanticism, they tell me, in loving a sad girl, because they feel vindicated when they can make them smile. There is an exquisite vulnerability in the performance of sadness and pain that they seek out, that is beautiful in itself. When women weep on television and in movies and books and even in songs, it is often an aesthetic affair: tears stream down their cheeks, their eyelashes are darkly matted with mascara, their mouths droop downwards in an irresistibly sad line that not only speaks of sorrow but also of beauty.

Beauty is pain. Beauty causes pain too. *She was so beautiful it hurt* is a phrase often heard. It describes the bone-deep ache we feel when we see a sunset or a city skyline at night. We ache because it is temporal, we ache because we cannot grasp it, we ache because we cannot comprehend it. But that is not the only pain caused by beauty.

A while ago, I wrote a poem called "Color." It's about a young girl and her pretty blonde doll that she keeps locked in a closet, scared that it will fly away. The girl in the poem is a little brown girl. As she grows older, the doll changes in her perception, it transforms; its whiteness is destroyed. As I illustrated it, I noticed (for the sake of convenience, I'd begun with the white doll and overlaid its features with brown paint and black hair) that the smiling expression of the doll in the first frame was rapidly disappearing. It wasn't that I was erasing her smile, it was just that her smile was naturally eroding under the weight of the full red lips, the dark brown skin I'd drawn on. The more color I added to the frame, the unhappier she grew.

As color seeped into her world, so did pain. Awareness of beauty hurts, but not as much as the awareness of ugliness, the awareness of something *lacking*. In Toni Morrison's tale, Pecola longs for blue eyes so much, suffers so much as a little black girl that "the matrix of her agony" is filled with death. The awareness of our lack of beauty forces us to strip away our skin, to bleach it, to cover up the darkness. Beauty is a construct, but who will tell that to those who deconstruct themselves in the search for beauty?

Like Pecola's friend, I scanned my own doll as a child for the signs of the beauty that had escaped me. I tried to dismember it, to find the secret of the desirability that had not escaped me. I locked my doll in a cupboard because her beauty hurt me. She was a doll; she faded into obscurity, but I remained.

Body

The tragedy of growing up is becoming aware of yourself.

When I was still a thin-armed child, I used to run home from school to watch *The Secret World of Alex Mack*. I loved the show. It was a story about a normal girl who got hit by a truck carrying nuclear chemicals. Like Peter Parker, she developed superpowers. One of them was that she could turn into a silver puddle. For a few moments, she was suspended as liquid—shimmering and free of a physical body.

When do you first notice your body? The strangeness of it, the shape of it?

Women talk about developing breasts or hips overnight—a sudden flowering of curves on a pubescent body. Sometimes, they write about getting their first period—that red and dramatic event. These things are meant to mark a transition. *This is when I became aware of what my body was. Now I know that it can bear children.* But I wasn't particularly disturbed by either of those events when they occurred in my life. I was a serene child; I liked to stay in and read. I liked to eat while reading too—two simple pleasures that came together naturally. The best snack was an apple because it was clean and self-contained. Or dark chocolate. Dark chocolate was the best because it was never cloying. You could taste the complexity of it, the smoke and ash of cocoa leaves mingled with sugar.

The day I first noticed my body was the day I was hunched over a book (devouring it and a bar of chocolate at an equally furious rate) when my uncle came in and told me, "You're going to be fat."

I looked up from my book in confusion. I was still far away, still in the places the book had made for me.

"You're going to be fat in a year," he said again, in the sort of voice you might use to announce that a fire had broken out, "if you don't control your portions of food. You shouldn't eat while reading. It's so easy to forget how much you're eating."

When do you first notice other people's bodies?

A few years ago, I saw a young boy comment on a stranger's size in an airplane. "Mummy, *look*, there's a fat lady in front of us." He didn't say it very loudly but he said it all the same, in a tone of absolute fascination. His mother turned scarlet and clapped a hand over his mouth before (presumably) hissing a lecture into his ear. *Wedon'tsaythingslikethatinpublicTimothy!*

When you're brown, you *do* say things like that in public. Nobody stops you.

I keep a running record of every comment, every offhand remark delivered on my body. Most of the comments came from the neighborhood aunties—the ones who were generous with their food as well as their criticisms. The auntie who comes over and pinches your side to feel how much you're filling out your skirt (because when you're a brown girl, your body is free to be pinched, squeezed, felt, and frisked). The auntie who asks about your bra size in a tone so intimate you want to cry. The auntie who says "you've certainly gained weight; how much do you weigh now?" without the slightest trace of embarrassment. As if it were routine information. As if she were entering it in a hospital ledger.

These are the behaviors we inherit.

There was a girl in our class who wasn't very popular. She was loud, squat, and dark-skinned, with constellations of acne. We used to call her "moti" behind her back because we saw the way her (always) too-tight white blouses strained against her flesh. We told ourselves it was a term of endearment. It wasn't entirely a lie. Desi culture encouraged nicknames like that—chasmish (one who wore spectacles), moti (who was fat), etc. We pointed out each other's most obvious physical traits so we were never in danger of forgetting our own.

After all, we rationalized that we were equal-opportunity offenders. If we called one girl fat, we called others skinny. Hips that caved inward, breasts that were not much more than little ridges on bones—these were not desirable to a people reared on images of curvaceous women standing beneath waterfalls. Aunties were just as prone to grab skinny girls and ask: "What's the matter? You don't get food at home? Try some of my chicken curry."

The chicken curry.

Our culture is not one that encourages dieting. We think nothing of using clarified butter, frying everything in oil, adding blocks of unsalted butter to our parathas and dipping them in gravies that are made mostly with cream. Even the chicken and paneer are cooked in butter. We eat the richest of foods and we never stop eating. Although Mallu food did not possess the milky richness of Punjabi food, it seemed to me that we were always eating without stint. When you went to your friends' houses, their mothers placed trays and platters of snacks full of fried chickpeas, plump discs of aloo, sweets so sugary they made your teeth ache, and glasses of rose syrup. They never asked if you were hungry.

"Aunty, I'm so full. I ate dinner at home, I can't," you protested as they ladled another hefty serving of curry on to your plate.

"Just a little bit," the aunty coaxed. "Don't you like it?"

To decline would have been to comment unfavorably on their cooking skills. And so, you ate.

It's hard to say exactly when I developed "body image issues." (The phrase sounds a trifle comical, "issues," like the issues of a magazine that keeps getting delivered to your house even as you try frantically to cancel your subscription.) I remember looking at a woodcut of Adam and Eve in the Garden of Eden and thinking, "If I had a body like that, I wouldn't mind being naked either." This struck me as an entirely appropriate reaction to a religious text.

I remember my girlfriends comparing their body weights as they picked at their school lunches (always floating in a puddle of oil). I remember my best friend's mother looking me up and down and asking, "How much do you weigh?" I remember my best friend saying, "You're tall, so you should try to be thin and then you can model!"

Of course, I wasn't thin. I have never been *thin*. Not past the age of eleven. With adolescence came puppy fat, a slow thickening of my body, the spreading of my hips. That was the first problem: my own size. The second problem was everybody else's. I was living in a country of extremely petite people. Sixteen may be the average American dress size, but you would be lucky to find a twelve in most Indian stores. I remember standing in a tailor's shop and being fitted for my cousin's wedding. The tailor took one look at me and said: "XXL."

I was flabbergasted at the number, at the fact that I was not a large, not an extra large, but an extra extra large. I felt like Augustus Gloop or an inflatable toy ready to burst. I took the dress he handed me—an ugly dress, far plainer than most Indian wedding outfits—and cried quietly in the changing room.

There were many moments like that. A quiet sobbing; a series of small humiliations. Trying to maintain a stoic expression as a relative told my mother, "Take her to a weight-loss clinic."

I thought wistfully of one of my favorite books, *Anne of Green Gables*, in which eleven-year-old Anne shouts at an older woman for calling her homely. I tried to imagine what would happen if I ever hit back at these aunties, ever told them, "It's not okay to comment on my body, please do not do that." It was too audacious to even imagine.

Of course, it wasn't only relatives or tailors who made such comments. People around me did that too, and so did the friends I suffered hopeless crushes on, and the (few) boys who were attracted to me. I learned that I had "love handles" from a boy I had hooked up with at nineteen. He had touched my sides and whispered that he didn't mind them, that he thought I was beautiful anyway.

The word sounded like it should have meant something lovely. Something tender. I was thankful that in the darkness, he couldn't see my face.

It's hard to say exactly when I developed an eating disorder. All I can tell you is that it started in high school and it never stopped. It wasn't anorexia, the most visible of eating disorders, not quite binge eating, and not even full-blown bulimia either. It was something else. EDNOS (eating disorder not otherwise specified).

Perhaps I caught the sickness at home but America made me sicker still.

Despite having lived in a culture of fat shaming, there was this saving grace: I'd grown up on images of voluptuous brown women. Our actresses were thin but not really *thin*. Thin meant that you weren't fat, that you had single-digit sizes. And then there was *thin*—beyond single-digit sizes. *Thin* was size zero—the kind of body that meant you never had to wear bras again. The kind of body that would be described as "waifish" or "gamine" by strangers. Audrey Hepburn. No less.

Kajol, the most beautiful woman I had ever seen at the time, wasn't *thin*. In *Dilwale Dulhaniya Le Jayenge*, when she runs into

Shah Rukh Khan's arms in a mustard field, she is beautiful, a picture of radiance and joy, but she isn't *skinny*. You cannot see her ribs in dresses. Her elbows aren't sharp; they don't look like they can cut Shah Rukh Khan when he hugs her.

None of the women in my life were thin. My mother was "normal," but she wasn't *thin*. My grandmother was positively, pleasantly plump. When she hugged me, I could feel that her flesh was expansive, generous. It felt like a benediction.

Nannayi is the Malayalam phrase for people who put on weight. It roughly translates to "you've become nice." You're nicely rounded. It was a compliment for people who were super skinny but had gained a little heft.

The only very thin women I grew up with were the dying ones. Sosamma Aunty, who had cancer. She was so thin that she looked like a comma. She was so tiny that she only seemed to occupy a fraction of whatever seat she was sitting on, which looked wrong to me. You shouldn't be able to fit another whole person in your seat, I remember thinking at the time.

I didn't know what the "ideal body" looked like, but I discovered it in whiteness.

The "it girls" or the supermodels—Kate Moss, Naomi Campbell, and Gia Carangi. With their enormous eyes, they arrested you from the page of a magazine. They were draped on couches, they slouched naked on ugly metal chairs and posed against industrial spaces. No matter which way they were posed, there was no roll of tummy visible, no unsightly wrinkle or curve except the curve of their own bodies (only a whisper of a body to clothe the bone, really).

But they were *models*, I told myself. It was an anomaly that they looked like that. They had won the genetic lottery. They could never become fat, not even if they ate mountains of Big Macs and drank a river of poisonously green Mountain Dew.

That kind of thinness was unnatural among regular bodies. That's what I told myself.

It was the year 2005 and I was headed to America to start college. It was also the year in which Nicole Richie and Lindsay Lohan catapulted to the very top of American teen culture.

I had not heard much about either of these women. Oh, of course, I knew Lindsay Lohan. Who didn't? All the girls in my tiny school in the hills knew LiLo. Linds. That lovable, effervescent teen queen. She had contagious energy. I almost thought of her as another Preity Zinta—she had the same dimples in her rounded face. I knew her body well;[1] I'd seen it in everything from *Freaky Friday* to *Mean Girls*. It was a beautiful body, truly. It was young and supple and just—a little!—just a little rounded. She was thin, but not *thin*.

So was Nicole Richie. Nicole I knew less of, but I'd seen *The Simple Life*. I'd thought it was hilarious—brilliant and funny—in revealing a Paris Hilton who was much sharper than people thought. (When Paris slipped into her dumb "valley girl" "that's hot!" upspeak, everybody was charmed—and that was a powerful tool.)

So, yes, there was Paris, slinking about in rhinestone tees and pink cowboy boots. Paris was another one of those girls so thin she could have been a model—she was thin enough to hook her flip phone into her (low-rise) jeans. But in sharp contrast to her body, all 5'11" glamorously thin inches of it, was Nicole Richie.

Nicole was pretty, definitely. She was even funnier than Paris, cracking deadpan jokes whenever the camera deigned to look her way. "Do we normally charge for this service?" she told her supervisor when a customer phoned to ask a question. Not two seconds later, she quipped, "We normally charge but you sound hot, so we'll do it for free."

Nicole was unquestionably the sidekick, the less pretty friend. Nicole wasn't fat—I couldn't imagine that they'd ever put a fat girl on TV—but she wasn't thin. She wasn't even as thin as Lindsay Lohan was. Sometimes, when the camera lingered on her, there was a little trace of pudge, of the curves that regular girls had. In fact, she was veering dangerously close to the edge of being a regular girl, of having a "normal" body.

In May 2005, the paparazzi leaked a shot of Lindsay and Nicole entering the Four Seasons Hotel. It was an astounding photo and has gone down forever in the annals of pop culture. It wasn't noteworthy for any particular reason; Lindsay or Nicole were not doing drugs. It wasn't who they were with or where they were going. It was simply the fact that they were both insanely, skeletally thin. Lindsay in her Marilyn red dress and blonde hair (though that was where the Marilyn resemblance ended) and Nicole in a crepe purple dress that floated over her body and found nothing to grasp on to. They had the bodies of children with nightmarishly large heads. They were mincing their way across grates in heels and they both looked satisfied. Happy. Laughing and smiling as they walked into the hotel. Who would not be if they were that thin? Go on, you can photograph me from whatever angle you want to. (Even from just beneath my chin, which is the pose most dreaded by celebrities.) I will never look anything other than *thin*.

I was amazed. The picture gave the lie to everything I had previously been thinking about bodies. I had been wrong after all. A thin body was achievable. Not just a thin body, but a *thin* body. Both Lindsay and Nicole had gone from their previous avatars to these bodies with (what looked to me like) zero effort. One day, thin. The next day, *thin*. A Jesus-level miracle wrought overnight.[2]

Hilary Duff (the other teen queen and Lindsay's sworn rival) was about to follow suit. Everywhere you looked, you were reminded of the inherent virtues of the whippet-thin body. Kate Bosworth. AnnaLynne McCord. Shenae Grimes. Kristin Cavallari. Jessica Alba. Mischa Barton.

Seventeen-year-old me was ashamed. I was about their age; I had dreams of being a spangled teen dream too. But when I surveyed myself (critical, unloving) I had something so different from their bodies that it was laughable.

It didn't help that I'd put on weight after coming to America. This was what a boy had warned me of in boarding school.

"America makes you fat," he'd said. "All those slices of pizza, all that junk food and late-night eating during study sessions. And no physical education classes any more to offset the food. Be careful."

Lo and behold, I'd become fat. I'd put on about fifteen or twenty pounds. It didn't show so much on my 5'7" frame. But I hated the way it made me look. I hated the way jeans cut into my flesh, the way sweatshirts stretched across my breasts. I hated the fact that I couldn't wear anything slinky without looking like a worm (not in a thin sense but in that my middle looked bisected).

I wish I could have said that I didn't know how it happened. It would have been nice to claim that there was something in the American air that had done it, that it were genes or puppy fat arriving late—anything but the shameful fact that I had been overeating every day for weeks and weeks and months and months.

I didn't have a weighing scale, didn't keep a food diary (yet), but I remember those meals. Those cycles of overconsumption. They are iridescent in my memory, impossible to remove. I dwell over them lovingly. I pick them apart delicately like cake crumbs.

Morning, breakfast. Waffles. Pancakes. (I preferred both to French toast, not liking the eggy feel of it.) Cereal, Lucky Charms, so rich with pink fuzzy marshmallows. Bacon or hash browns. Those special Sunday breakfasts with slices of angel food cake heaped with chocolate chips and whipped cream, carved in slices so you could pour strawberry compote through the cracks. To-go cups everywhere because you were running late for class. You never had time to linger over breakfast, did you? Better take something to eat later. Even in class, maybe. Nobody minded if you ate in class or where you ate. America!

Lunch. Wherever you wanted to eat lunch—whichever dining hall was closest to your last class. Lunch was my least favorite meal, but poring over Greek plays made me starving hungry, and so I dutifully wolfed down a whole sandwich with chips (not an apple, never an apple). Of course, dessert, ice cream perhaps. Or fruit "salad" that was essentially strawberry pie without the crust.

Some more studying—glorious hours of a mellow October whiled away indoors—and then it was time for dinner. Early by desi standards: 7 P.M. So much food for dinner, a hobbit-like spread. Mini pizzas baked and pressed neatly into squares; whole pans of lasagna, enough to make Garfield groan; vaguely Chinese beef 'n' broccoli with glistening carrot discs and golden niblets of corn. A glutinous feast, but the day's consumption was far from over.

M&C's. A uniquely Mount Holyoke tradition: milk and cookies at 10:30 P.M. Because the dinner we'd eaten at seven wasn't enough to hold us through the night! We would pile special Chef Jeff cookies on to dessert plates (the only small plates we used in college) and crunch our way through them while doing our homework. A tall glass of milk, white and innocent. Full fat and tasting so different in America than it had at home. Enough milk to put us to sleep. We snored, our bellies full.

And that, of course, was ignoring the alcohol.

So much alcohol, even though none of us were old enough to drink. We found ways to do it still—we coaxed and cajoled our seniors into picking bottles up for us when they went to the liquor store. We made fake IDs or borrowed other people's (I would always hold up my classmate Nazish's ID to the bouncer, confident he wouldn't notice that she was only 5'1").

We drank in our dorms, watching episode after episode of *America's Next Top Model*. We drank in other people's dorms—

slightly sheepish invitees to all-lesbian parties that were too grown
up for us. We drank in the houses on UMass's Frat Row, watching
bulky redheaded boys dive into pools of Jell-O as if life held no
purer enjoyment. We drank in smoky basements at Amherst and
got so drunk we threw up in the bushes outside. Beer—endless
supplies of beer—and Stolichnaya vodka, and sugary Monkey Bar
cocktails on the nights we made it into Monkey Bar.

"Julie, you know those LIITs are, like, a thousand calories
apiece," said one toweringly skinny Amherst girl to another. She
flicked a sheet of perfectly ironed blonde hair over her shoulder, it
landed like glass. "*I'm* gonna order a skinny vodka seltzer." And I
would too in the hope that it would disappear my fat. But I might
as well have ordered those Long Island Iced Teas, sweating in their
enormous pitchers. Because we weren't like the Julies, going back
to a frat house to hook up with whichever boy looked the most like
slabs of muscle in his cranberry polo. No, we had the refuge of food
and so we piled into taxicabs that took us to Friendly's or Wendy's
or Denny's—so many y's—and ordered the Bloomin Onion Special
Funky Fresh Delite with *extra* fries and extra *extra* meat sides, easy
on the mustard and heavy on the mayo, if you please.

"Y'all reckon y'all gonna finish that?" the waitress would ask,
snapping her gum. "That's a trucker-size meal and y'all don't look
big enough to put that away."

"Oh, trust me, we'll manage."

We didn't, but we came close. We had to leave a few sad,
gluey fries and the bread buns of the burgers. We didn't walk out
of there, said one of my friends, we *rolled*.

There was something glorious about overconsumption. I'd
studied in school that if everyone lived like an American—had an
American-size carbon footprint—we would need four more earths
to sustain us.[3] They were consuming that much of its resources. A
defiant "fuck you" to everybody else.

I gave myself up to it. Why not eat pretzels mindlessly or Little Debbie's Cakes? Why not power your way through a bag of Hot Cheetos or Funyuns while studying for finals? After all, we were in the land of plenty. We were only eating as the characters did on American sitcoms. (I conveniently put aside the fact that those characters, like Rory Gilmore, never seemed to gain weight.)

Perhaps, if I'd felt prettier—or, perhaps, if I'd felt like my body was worthy of being cherished and loved—I wouldn't have fallen into the patterns that I did. But, I was a brown girl in a wasteland of blinding whiteness and it never occurred to me that I myself was worthy of being cherished and loved.

I said I was acting out when I slept with people whose names I didn't remember. I told myself I was being wild and free! I was living the life that I'd dreamed of! The small, stifled life of Kerala was light years away from the scandal and sex of Sigma Tau Gamma. Or so I told myself. One night, on my way to the bathroom in an Amherst dorm, I took the wrong turn and got locked out.

It was an icy night and I started feeling the freeze almost immediately. Amherst doors were operated by a code that I didn't know and I was only wearing a bathrobe. Luckily, two girls who were going outside for a cigarette stumbled into me. I asked them for the code.

"You, uh, you don't go here, do you?" they asked amusedly.

"No."

They looked delicately at my attire.

"Here visiting a boy?"

"Yes." There was no way of denying the obvious—I was there for a hook-up. It felt useless to camouflage this information.

"Which suite is he in?"

I tried to think. I didn't remember.

"What's his name?"

Blank.

"I think it starts with A . . . I think it starts with A," I said in a tiny voice.

After that, the girls studiously avoided my eyes. They let me in and walked away quietly. There was something so pathetic about what was happening, about the fact that I was there to have sex with a man whose name I could not remember. Had I delighted in this fact, had I laughed and said in a breezy Samantha Jones-esque way—"I'm here for a dick appointment, ladies! Who cares what his name is!"—they would have laughed too, been equally delighted. That version of me would have been a girl enjoying sex without shame. This version of me felt . . . small. Desperate.

In comparison, my need to feel desirable—even though I had not been desired by the man whose dorm I came out of—was as vast as the ocean. If anybody wanted to sleep with me, I slept with them. I even thanked them in my head for wanting to sleep with me. I genuinely wondered why they did. Why? Was it some kind of punishment for them, some way of "slumming it?"

After all, I was not only a plain girl, not only a chubby plain girl, but also a *brown* chubby plain girl. So many burdens on one body.

I remember the white boy looked me over like I was livestock and said: "Can I ask you a question? What color are your nipples?" Still, I was grateful for the attention. I would have been grateful for any attention. The pity of it.

* * *

What was reflected in the glass was about the most adorable, the most dazzling sixteen-year-old girl imaginable [. . .] She spun around to show off a stunning figure without an extra ounce visible anywhere [. . .] She fluttered long eyelashes over almond-shaped eyes the blue-green of the Caribbean [. . .] Both girls had the same shoulder-length, sun-streaked blond hair, the same sparkling blue-green eyes, the same perfect skin. Even the tiny dimple in Elizabeth's left cheek was duplicated in her younger sister's—younger by four minutes. Both girls were five feet six on the button and generously blessed with spectacular, all-American good looks.

This is the description that opens *Double Love*, Francine Pascal's bestselling series about the twins of Sweet Valley. It is also a description that is repeated in practically every book since, in case you were in danger of forgetting what Jessica and Elizabeth Wakefield looked like. They were perfect size sixes, chanted every book right at the beginning.[4] So was their mother, Alice Wakefield (the possessor of "a youthful figure"). So was Lila Fowler, Jessica's best friend. So were Amy Sutton, Cara Walker, Dana Fowler, and all the girls at Sweet Valley High (SVH), apparently.

The only not-slim one was Robin Wilson. Robin, who first appeared in Sweet Valley High #4, *Power Play*. Robin was desperate to join Jessica's group, Pi Beta, but was rejected out of hand by Jessica. "That fat wimp!", "That butterball!", "That tub of lard!" shrieked Jessica, letting us know just how repulsive she found Robin.

Tremendously hurt at her exclusion, Robin decided to take up running. Day after day, she ran five miles on the school track. She began to follow a spartan diet. Elizabeth (who was described as kinder than her sister) noted that Robin's lunch was "[. . .] only lettuce leaves, tomato slices and a hard-boiled egg." Under this punishing regime, Robin began losing weight. A ton of weight. Finally, she was transformed, butterfly style, into one of the most popular, beautiful, and stylish girls at Sweet Valley High. She was named co-captain of the cheerleading squad—the highest social accolade in the world of SVH.

If she could do it, why couldn't I?

I had all the tools at my disposal, after all. I had the whole Internet. I had thousands of pro-ana[5] and pro-mia[6] forums to learn from. On these sites, girls huddled around each other, forming protective circles. I imagined them at a table in a high-school cafeteria, pulling their sleeves over their nearly translucent wrists. Denuding their burgers of buns; carefully picking out the croutons in their salads.

These sites were full of tips.

This is how you binge eat in private. This is how you eat a single meal per day. This is how you go on a liquid cleanse (did you know Beyoncé did it for a movie premiere?). This is how you make yourself throw up everything you binged. This is how you hide food in your napkin when you're eating with people. This is how you take cold baths to burn more calories. This is how you run the AC all night long so you shiver and your muscles burn off more calories. This is how you tell people that you "already ate" or that you're "feeling too sick to eat." This is how you fast and this is how you compulsively exercise. This is how you wear baggy clothes so nobody notices you're losing weight. This is how you move food around on your plate so it looks like you're eating. This is how you suck on a single lollipop all day long when you're starving hungry. This is how to do it. Take notes.

It became impossible for me to eat anything without obsessing over it. I did complex mental calculations in my head—if a burger at MHC's Café Blanchard was 370 calories but I scraped off the sauce and ate it without the bun, how much would it run to? I drank black coffee in the evenings instead of eating dinner. I woke up in the mornings feeling faint and nauseous from not having eaten since the day before. I exercised compulsively, running mile after dreary mile, spending an hour at a time on the elliptical machine. I refused to go to any restaurants that didn't list calorie counts on their menus.

When I *did* go out, I ordered salads without any dressing, nuts, cheese, or meat. No raisins or fruit either—they were full of sugar.

"That's just going to be leaves," said one waiter, looking at me with pity, like he was embarrassed for me. "You know that's nothing but leaves."

It pains me to record that I was a bad anorectic. However hard I tried, I could not, like some girls, will myself into not eating. At the most, my not-eating stints lasted a couple of meals. I remember going down to the kitchen after one particularly bad day where I hadn't eaten much. It was well after M&C's and there was nothing set out on the clean tables except saltines and tiny, sterile packages of oyster crackers. Six to a pack. I methodically assembled twenty of those packs and dipped them in the bottles of olive oil and balsamic vinegar that the kitchen staff never removed. I ate my way through the packs, unable to register any taste at all.

When the meal was over, I got up and shovelled my plate into the bin. I wondered what somebody would think if they saw it—those twenty empty packs of crackers and saltines. It was as if a homeless person had broken into the college. I wiped my mouth with a napkin, it was slick with oil.

I wanted to laugh at myself. I had recently read Portia de Rossi's memoir about anorexia, *Unbearable Lightness: A Story of Loss and Gain*. Portia—whom I'd previously only known from *Ally McBeal*[7]—had commendable will power, I told myself. She had "dieted" herself down to an astonishing eighty-something pounds. She ran on the treadmill through lunch and ate quarter cups of yogurt and *I Can't Believe It's Not Butter* cooking spray without complaining about these nauseating meals. Compared to her, I was a joke. When I dieted—even lightly—I dreamed about food. Potatoes, in particular. I swam in mounds of mashed potato. Creamed potatoes au gratin. Patatas bravas. Aloo tikki on small plates that street vendors in India gave you. Fluffy french fries. Potato paradise. It would have been hilarious if it hadn't been so depressing. (I always woke up just before I could eat the meal in my dreams.)

If I dieted for two meals, I cracked on the third. I had no self-control, definitely not the kind of obsessive self-control you needed to be an anorexic. I wasn't even good enough at anorexia to be thin. (Never *thin*.)

Very well. If I couldn't be anorexic, I would try harder to be bulimic.

* * *

I don't know where the idea first came to me. It's difficult to say—one night I might have been throwing up from drinking too much. The night that my German friend told me that mixing beer and vodka was normal, that people did it all the time. (I was so green that I believed her and mixed beer and vodka in my red Solo cup.) Perhaps, I noticed that I was also throwing up my dinner. Perhaps, I noticed that it was an easy way to get rid of the food.

I took to bulimia in a way I had never taken to anorexia. *Pro-mia*. It was made for me, I thought, because I was someone who enjoyed excess instead of restraint. I didn't want to skip meals, I wanted to eat three at once. I already knew what it felt like to overeat; this would merely be an extension of that. Bulimia meant that I could embrace America's excesses! I didn't need to count calories, I could order anything I wanted to off the menu at cheap chain restaurants. All I needed to do was make sure I followed the meal with ice cream. Yogurt. Soft serve. In a pinch, a creamy, dreamy milkshake. Anything to make sure the food came up easily.

I formed the habit—one I have to this day—of noting where the bathroom was anywhere I went. How crowded was it? Were the stalls private? Might someone come in at any time or would I be guaranteed privacy for at least three minutes? All I needed was three minutes. One to lock the door and bend over the stall, one to stick my finger down my throat until the food came up (*great heaving gobs of food, disgusting, disgusting, disgusting*), and one to clean up.

I made sure to always have breath mints in my purse. I wore too much perfume, praying that nobody would catch the dank smell of vomit lingering on my jacket. Other than that, it was remarkably easy to hide the evidence. My eyes were only bloodshot for a minute. I would wait in front of the mirror, take my hair out of its elastic, apply another prim coat of lipstick, and it was done. I would stroll out of the loo, nonchalant.

If I were in a restaurant, I would be too ashamed to meet the eyes of the waiters as I walked past them. Waiters have a way of knowing which of their patrons have eating disorders (the food left in the napkin, the telltale vomit flecks on the side of the toilet). I imagined how they thought of me: wasteful, irresponsible, throwing away a $24 entrée because I didn't have the self-control to not eat it in the first place.

It wasn't always so simple. Sometimes, there would be people in the next stall and I'd have to wait for them to leave. I couldn't risk them hearing me. (Only a bulimic knows how loud the sound of vomiting is.)

Sometimes, there were too many people waiting in line and I couldn't throw up at all. In that event, I would panic. I would calculate how many calories I had put into my body. *Idiotic, stupid, reckless.* Calories that I couldn't get out. Now they would be absorbed into my bloodstream, slowly. One by one. Making more fat cells. *More* fat deposits on my fat body.

I found and reread the book *A Little Stranger* by Candia McWilliam. I'd first read it when I was a child, and I remembered it was about eating disorders. A young, slightly plump nanny falls for the dad of the house, a well-worn trope, thus setting up a rivalry between the wife and the nanny. But in a clever working of the narrative, McWilliam makes the wife an overeater and the nanny bulimic.

> My glowing feasts were celebrations of being a child. I lifted from myself the weight of thought as I donned that precious fat [. . .] It was so beautiful; how could it do harm? At the same time, Margaret was carrying out her inverted worship of the same god.[8]

I was struck by the perfection of this metaphor. If the narrator found food holy, if she likened overeating to a holy act, so too was throwing up a holy act.

After all, we had to get on our knees for it.

I was careful not to overdo it. I knew how stomach acids could corrode enamel and I didn't want to be fitted with a set of false teeth at thirty. In *A Little Stranger*, the narrator describes how Margaret grows hirsute, how her spittle becomes thick. I was terrified of growing hair all over my previously unhairy (for a brown girl) arms and legs. Becoming a budget Sasquatch.

> If the fat wish to be a shadow of their former selves, the sickly thin wish to be the flesh of their future selves, not a flesh fed by nourishment, but the plump, taut, muscled and yet tender flesh of romance, ready to be carved. While they reject and vomit food, for what are these girls paying, these girls wanting to be hollow? What fantastic connection has been made between daydreams of beauty and romance and that life of bitter spitting?[9]

I closed the book. It was too real; it made me feel sick. McWilliam could not understand that "connection between romance and spitting"—all she could do was remark on its oddity. But I could.

My bathroom-worship did pay off. My body did change. To some extent. Bulimia combined with judicious dieting and cutting out carbs meant that I was losing weight. I could see the numbers on the scale going down—154, 150, 149, 147, 140, 138 . . . 133 . . .

Not enough—never enough—but I slimmed down to a size where I was now acceptable, even desirable. I pushed the XXL dresses to the back of my closet and replaced them with mediums. I no longer dreaded flights back to India. The aunties who had casually made such cruel remarks in the past were now obsessed with asking me how I "did it."

One of them cornered me in a hallway and patted my midriff as though she was airport security. "What are you doing? What's your secret? Is it keto? Tell me!" she commanded. "My daughter needs to lose weight too."

I smiled. "Oh, just eating healthy and exercising, you know." *Restricting, fasting, counting, occasionally abusing Adderall because it killed my appetite, cleansing, binging, purging, lying, lying, lying.*

I thought of all the brown daughters nagged about their weight by their mothers. Always being put on fad diets, always being told, "You know, that samosa has 350 calories. Would you like some sprouts instead?" while their brothers reached for a second and a third. I felt tears spring to my eyes. I wanted to cry—I *was* crying—for her daughter.

"If you can lose weight, so can she."

In her mind, I was a success story. A chubby girl who lost weight in obedience. A neat coda to a distressing tale. I was an argument in favor of plain speaking: "If you don't tell people that they've gained weight, they won't have any incentive to lose it, no?"

No. They won't. Better by far to tell our women and girls to lose weight, even if they develop eating disorders in the process. A brown girl who loves her body—her flawed, chubby, stretchmark-ridden, acne-pitted, hyper pigmented body—is an anomaly. A body-confident brown girl is a *problem*. What do we brown girls know about self-love? Who is teaching us to love ourselves?

In 2014, a young Indo-Canadian poet broke on to the *New York Times* bestsellers' list with her debut collection, *Milk and Honey*. Her name was Rupi Kaur, and she would go on to outsell Homer. Yes, *that* Homer.

Her runaway success left the literary world (and much of the regular world) baffled. White writers and critics pored over her poems to try and decipher the secret of her popularity. Kaur's poems were laughably simple, often only two or three lines (in lower case, without punctuation) with simple black and white drawings next to them. They were originally published on Instagram, not in any sort of chapbook or poetry journal. A typical Kaur poem:

if you were born with
the weakness to fall
you were born with
the strength to rise

The backlash was swift and inevitable. A flurry of articles deriding Kaur's poetry began to appear: "This quiz is proof Kaur writes bad poetry,"[10] "Rupi Kaur's bad poems shouldn't worry us,"[11] "Rupi Kaur's poetry needs workshopping,"[12] and even "Instagram poet Rupi Kaur seems utterly uninterested in reading books."[13] Shade upon shade, much of it from older white people who seemed befuddled that a person who is unabashedly literary could be the reigning queen of popular poetry. She became a joke of sorts on social media—people would post three or four arbitrary lines and end with her trademark, "*rupi kaur*."

And yet, Kaur is loved. I watch her in person at the Jaipur Literature Festival 2018 and marvel at the crowd that has gathered from all over India. She sways, a slender figure dressed in a soft pink kaftan; her stage presence is hypnotic. She recites poem after poem that calls upon girls to love themselves and I think: here is the secret. The key to Kaur's appeal is that she is preaching self-love to brown girls. She is telling them—no matter the form, no matter the quality of her poems—that they are beautiful, that they are worthy.

It is not something we have been taught. "*Love* yourself." "Treat yo'self." "Self-care is important." These are not things that are easily come by for brown girls. These may be white girl mantras, but they are not ours. How many of us stumble out of college dorms or sleep with boys we don't know because we think that anything given to us is too much?

Every brown girl who loves herself is a revolutionary. The truth is that every brown girl who is at home in her own body (despite its hairiness, despite its unruliness, despite its squatness or stretchmarks) is a performer of miracles.

I want to be optimistic. I want to say that at least *some* things have gotten better. We no longer live in an era where extreme thinness is the only beauty ideal. We now have Kim Kardashian, Kylie Jenner, and the rest of their clan. And yet, have they freed us from the burden of thinness or have they added another layer to it? For now, we are expected to be body-positive. We are told (hollow injunction!) to "love" our flawed bodies even though they do not resemble the aerodynamic, perfectly engineered "thickness" that the new celebrities represent. White girls with the (surgeon-bought) bodies of black girls and Latinas.

And more than ever before, these beauty ideals are thrust on us. A fourteen-year-old brown girl growing up in Gujarat with a smartphone can download Instagram and stare longingly at pictures of other fourteen-year-old girls who do not look like fourteen-year-old girls at all. All day long, she can immerse herself in the world of crop tops and contour and IG "baddies" that do not look like any Indian girl she knows. How is it enough to preach self-love and body positivity in the face of this onslaught? Brown girls are intelligent. They know what they—what *we*—are being told.

I wish I could close this with a happy ending or at least a cathartic one. What can I tell you now about my body or my eating disorder? I want to write that I lost weight and stopped thinking about it for good. I wish I could tell you that I no longer have body issues, that I no longer skip meals or go on ridiculous diets. I am at an "ordinary weight." I exercise when I can and I eat healthy. Should that not be enough? Must I spend the rest of my life standing in front of the mirror, moving my weight from foot to foot? Will tyrannical dressing room mirrors always leave me in tears? I want so badly to be able to focus on my work. I hunger to not obsess over my body. No more, in this life, in this *duniya*. I have endured so much already.

If I could draw a line under my weight and move on to the next page, I would. But that would not be the truth, and I want to tell you that eating disorders don't disappear, they merely recede into the background of your life.

If you're lucky, they stay in the background. Some days—if you're *really, truly*, lucky—they let you enjoy food without thinking about them. As if you don't have a body at all but are as weightless and free as a small silver puddle in the gloom.

III
LOVE

Dump Him

Picture this:

The interior of a dimly lit restaurant in the evening. *Two girls having an intimate conversation at the bar.*

Ängsö:[1] OK, so you know I adore Frajen, but oh my God, this is the limit!

Arnholma: I know! Oh my God! Why doesn't she just get it? Dump him, girl.

Ängsö: I think it's just unfair on us, you know? I feel like we should be getting paid for being her therapists. Every time he does her dirty, who has to pick up the pieces? US.

Arnholma: Remember that one time, at Tosterö's birthday, when he caught a cab home without telling her? Who does that? He is *literally* a sociopath.

Ängsö: Every time we tell Frajen to dump him, she promises us that she will. And then we tell her she could do so much better and remind her of that weird earring phase he had. And she's like, "Yeah, you're right, you're right. I know you're right." But then the next weekend they're jointly RSVPing to Malm's BBQ even though she said it was going to be super cazh. And it turns out she told him what we said about the earring and we come off as the uber bitches of the scenario.

Arnholma: Exactly! Every single time she says she'll dump him.

Ängsö: And then she doesn't.

Arnholma: Never!

Ängsö: Never!

* * *

It is a truth universally acknowledged that nothing strains female friendships quite as much as bad boyfriends.

I used to know this girl—let's call her Sonya—who was dating a terrible man. Let's call him Nikhil. He was a DJ, which ought to have been red flag #1. DJs are the root canals of people.[2]

When we were introduced at a party, he refused to look me in the eye.

"Nikhil, thisismyfriendwhoItoldyouabout!" said Sonya. If she were any more buoyant, she might have floated away.

"I need a beer," he said, and went to a corner of the room where there was no beer. Sonya gripped my arm.

"He's so funny! He's allergic to people so he's always doing funny things like that. I have no idea how he became a DJ."

"Wow," I said.

"Do you think we look good together? I love how we look together."

"Yeah. Yeah, you know, he seems cool. He's got that, uh, silent, cool, thing going on." I prayed these words were enough. I'd never been good at lying.

Over time, the first cracks in their relationship began to show.

Nikhil never confided in Sonya. He never wanted to see her during daytime. He had no work ethic at all—unless Sonya wanted to do something that he didn't want to do, during which he would tell her he was "too busy to hang out." (He invariably described their relationship as "hanging out." As in: *We're hanging out right now. No, I'm not hanging out with anybody else.*)

He was also cheating on her.

I have a grudging respect for men who work hard to cover up their cheating. The kind of men who go to bars where they won't be seen and who delete all their text messages. Nikhil, alas, was not one of these men. When Sonya snooped on his phone, she found the proof right away. Apparently, he'd been seeing not one, not two, not three, but four other women.

Four!

"I just can't understand," she said in a high-pitched voice on the phone, "when he has the time to see *five* women."

"He must be less lazy than I thought," I said without thinking. "I mean—that's terrible. What did you do? Was the breakup awful?"

"Well, I was upset at first—naturally!—but then he told me that he was in the process of breaking up with those other women because I was the one he really liked. So then I felt like I'd overreacted a little . . . *He* felt horrible about it, by the way. You should have seen his face when I started crying. He had to deal with all my emotions and stuff at that moment, you know." She said "emotions" in the same way airport security might say "explosive devices."

"Yeah. Wow. That must have been hard for him," I said in the most neutral voice I could manage. "Dealing with your emotions and all."

"I mean, I was in the wrong too, you know? He pointed out that I shouldn't have been snooping on his phone.[3] I should have trusted him," she said, sounding like a bunny with a bad cold.

I pointed out that he had given her literally zero reasons to trust him, but it was too late—she had landed squarely in Denial and I knew there was no return flight from Denial. Not for a good long time.

"Yeah. Oh my God, I just saw the time. I'm late. For a thing."

"What thing?"

I tried to think of something I'd been invited to recently that she'd hate. "Uh, it's a women-only slam poetry session."

There was silence at the other end.

"Can I come?"

Jesus Christ, the bitch was desperate.

"I, uh, yeah, it's by invite only. I wish you could, I really do. But just stay at home, okay? And do something fun. Order some Thai food. And I'll . . . I gotta go. So we'll talk later." I hung up and lay back on my bed without feeling the slightest trace of guilt.

In my defence, being the single girlfriend demands a certain degree of unselfishness. You have to listen to many, MANY, many stories about the minutiae of other people's relationships. (*"He said something super mean that one time but it could have meant this other thing, which isn't mean, so I can't figure out which one it is and now I don't know if I have the right to be mad!"*)

When you're single, people are only interested in your bad dating stories, which they can live vicariously through. They expect you to have less to talk about, which is profoundly unfair—I mean, what about the state of your succulents? Don't they want to know about that?

Eventually, you come to know your friend's boyfriend intimately. It's almost as if *you* are dating him. You know how he kisses and you know his texting style and you know what he said to the waitress at the restaurant. You resent your friend for making you hear these stories. You resent her for making you say the same thing over and over again: *dump him.*

The solution's so *simple* to you, so *obvious*. It's like somebody complaining that they keep burning down their apartment. *Well,* you say, *maybe you should stop setting it on fire.* After giving them this advice for the first dozen times and being consequently ignored, you get fed up. You want to leave them alone with their rubble.

At first, I put it gently to Sonya: "Maybe you need some time to reflect on your relationship. You know, to take a break and really think about what you want and if he's giving it to you." I didn't point out that this would take her five seconds and that the answer was no.

The second time, I put it strongly.

"I feel like this is done," she said, sniffling. "This is over. I can't stand to be in the same room with him any more."

I felt thrilled.

"Can I say something? I never really liked him."

"Really?" she said.

"There's his hairstyle," I said. She cracked a smile, but I had just begun:

"And I feel like you go to all his events but he never shows up for you in the same way. With anything! He's never as interested in your life as you are in his. And the money thing. Don't you always pay for him? He doesn't do anything for you, Son. If you made a list of things you did for each other, the ledger would be so unbalanced. It's not fair. These are the times we should be focusing on ourselves, you know, on our careers, and we're wasting all this time with these mediocre men who don't have anything to offer us except mediocre sex. It's so frustrating!"

She fell quiet for a beat. *Shit.*

"Well, he's still making it as a DJ. You don't make a lot of money when you're just starting off."

"Sure."

"There were some good times. He helped me wash my hair when I broke my arm—"

"Of course," I said, wanting more than anything to end this horrible, horrible conversation.

"I'll think about it," she said.

I knew she wouldn't.

It developed into a cycle. She would call me crying. I would invite her over to talk about it. I would tell her she had to dump him. ("At this point, you don't have any other *choice*, Son. I hate seeing you so unhappy.") She always agreed. ("I know, I know.") But a few weeks later, there she'd be, right back on my couch, crying.

After one of these sessions, I felt the need to have a venting session of my own. I called my other friends and we talked about how tired we were of listening to her. The conversations always started with a disclaimer: "I love Sonya so much, but—"

I started to avoid her. I felt this was fair. She knew exactly what I thought of her dilemma—I'd only told her 107 times. I couldn't understand why it wasn't working.

In the movies, there's always the sassy girl who *tells it like it is.* This character is often a woman of color, usually the protagonist's best friend. She doesn't seem to have a real job. She's barely a real person. All she does is sit on bar stools and say things like "Girl, you *have* to get laid!" and "Dump him!" She believes in tough love. I imagine her going up to overweight strangers and snatching their breakfast pastries "This is *440* calories! You don't need this!" In real life, this character would be locked up. Or at least be very, very unpopular. Everybody is far more aware of their weaknesses than we imagine.[4] I'm not quite sure what "tough love" means, but it often seems to involve pointing out these weaknesses and making people feel bad about themselves.

If shaming people were a sure-fire strategy, nobody would ever smoke cigarettes. And the Nikhils of the world would be in danger of extinction. Unfortunately for all of us, it doesn't work that way.

I'm not sure when Sonya figured out that I was tired of hearing about her relationship, but she did. Gradually, she stopped talking to me about Nikhil. During a conversation with another friend, I mentioned how happy I was that she'd moved on.

"Oh, she's still seeing him," said the friend. "She just isn't talking to you about it."

"What? That's so unfair," I cried. "I've been here for her for months and months. Why wouldn't she tell me?"

"I don't know," said my friend simply. "I think she's embarrassed to admit it. I mean, she's not stupid—she knows she's, like, being a bad feminist or whatever—but she says she can't help it because she loves him."

It was as if somebody had clobbered me with an anvil in a *Road Runner* cartoon. Never before had it occurred to me that anybody could actually *love* Nikhil. (I had assumed his mother was the only one and even then it was only because she didn't know him well enough.)

What if *I* were in love with someone who made me unhappy? Maybe I wouldn't be able to let them go so easily. Maybe it would take me 100 crying sessions until I was ready to let go. Maybe I needed someone to listen to me without judgment till I was ready.

It struck me that I hadn't done this for Sonya. All I had done was wait for her to finish whatever she was telling me and then burst out: "You have to dump him!" Instead of doing all the things I could have done to cheer her up, I'd chosen to beat her over the head with "just dump him." She was telling me: "Hey, I'm sad because I can't seem to do this thing," and I was making her feel worse about not being able to do it. No wonder she'd stopped being honest with me.

I couldn't even remember letting her cry without an *I told you so* seeping into the conversation. In my next life, I'd be reincarnated as a cockroach.

In an effort to right the karmic scales, I took Sonya out to dinner two weeks later. She talked and talked about everything but Nikhil. She talked about all the great men she was meeting.

"Aren't you still seeing Nikhil?" I said, in the most nonchalant tone I could manage.

"Well," she said, a little pink in the face, "yeah, I'm still seeing him." Emboldened by my lack of response, she went on: "I know, I know. We'll break up eventually—I know I have to. But we have great times too. Did you know he knows how to beatbox? He taught me a little."

She pursed her lips and produced a hoarse clucking noise that made other people look around in alarm. It sounded nothing like anything I'd ever heard. Then she looked at me in an expectant way that broke my heart.

Not everybody can handle tough love all the time, I thought. Maybe some people need a softer love. Something to get them through the days until they are stronger.

"That's amazing," I said, and—you know what—I meant it.

Appendix: Some Types of Desi Fuckboys

1) The Heir

Heirs in other countries pretend not to work, but the Indian heir is often employed (unfortunately taking a job away from the people who really need it).

He pretends he got the job on his own.

Knows everybody's father. And their father. And their father's father.

Goes on an illegal safari with his uncle (an MP).

Has never heard the word *no* in his life and this has helped him develop a monstrous carapace of entitlement (a high "5" on the Levenson Psychopathy Scale).

Probably killed someone and buried the body in his estate in Sainik Farms.

Has an estate in Sainik Farms.

Genus: Birla, Tata, Jindal

Markings: Audi, BMW, Turnbull & Asser bespoke shirts

Sounds: "My driver did it."

2) The JNU Student

He might be attending any university in any city in India but he is most commonly referred to as "that JNU type."

Thinks wearing a kurta is civic participation. (He doesn't necessarily vote.)

Always "just finishing up" his PhD.

Has been in grad school for nine years.

You'll have to pay for his Masala Maggi and, in the winter, his Old Monk with Coke.

Dating him means lying in his hostel room for hours, watching shitty French art films, and smoking cheap charas. Once he gets stoned, he'll tell you, "Something real deep, bro. Something real deep."

Genus: MPhil

Markings: Jute bag, owlish glasses

Sounds: "Well, according to Žižek—"

3) The Slam Poet

When he's introduced to you, he says something you don't understand, like: "You are the petrichor of people." You are not quite sure what this means, but you feel it is not as much of a compliment as he thinks it is.

His poetry is inevitably terrible. So terrible, in fact, that you'd rather read the nutrition facts on a packet of Lay's Magic Masala.

You'll have to pay for his Lay's Magic Masala. He never has any money because, "There isn't any money in poetry, apparently." (You want to ask him how he can explain Rupi Kaur then.)

R*pi K*ur is a forbidden subject.

You should send him nudes because he's "sex positive."

Says it's feminist to send him nudes.

Once he gets drunk, he'll tell you why it's actually feminist to have a threesome with you and your best friend.

Genus: Unemployed

Markings: An unwashed beard

Sounds: "This reminds me of something I've been working on—luckily, I have it right here on my phone so I can perform it to the group!"

4) The Uncle

Twenty-seven going on fifty-seven, right down to the Nehru jacket, the uncle-bod, and the pro-BJP opinions.

Incessantly talks about how much he made at his law practice during the last fiscal quarter.

Dating him is like dating the uncle from your gym who gets on a treadmill, wheezes for five minutes, and then comes over to explain how you should use free weights.

Has almost certainly never gone down on a woman.

Even your father thinks he's boring.

Always orders the same thing at restaurants. "We'll have one plate of seekh kebabs, one butter chicken, one naan, one shahi paneer, and one kulfi. And—no, make that two plates of butter chicken. Best to stick to butter chicken."

Genus: Golf Club

Markings: Poorly fitted pants, a mid-range car, holding an FT

Sounds: *mansplaining intensifies*

5) The Britjabi

Always hunts in packs. If you're dating him, you're dating his entire crew. (They roll sixteen deep.)

From London by way of Ludhiana. Or Canada by way of Amritsar. Or New York by way of Chandigarh. Develops suspiciously thick NRI accent after two months.

Orders Red Bull at the club like a deranged person.

Strange psychosexual relationship with his mother (like every other Indian man, but more so).

Manages a bar. Manages a club. Manages a chain of restaurants in shady areas of the city.

Shares your nudes with "his boys."

Will call you "bro" right after sex.

Will slut-shame you immediately after you break up.

Genus: Dhillon Singh Dhillon

Markings: Ed Hardy gear

Sounds: "Let's go Goa, bro. Massive scenes happening there. Let's go London. Let's go Las Vegas. Lespardy, bro. Get girls along, bro. LESPARDYYYYYYYYYYYYYYYYYYYYYYYYYYYYYYYYYYY YYYYYYYYYYYYYYYYYYYYYYYYYYY BROOOOOOOO OOOOOOOOOOOOOOOOOOOOOOOOOOOOOOOO."

6)   The Boy Who Thinks He's Black

Has "n**ga" on his Instagram handle. Drops the n-word more frequently than it's used in a Quentin Tarantino film.

Captions every photo "squad," "gang," or "murda bidness." "We don't catch feelings, we catch bodies n**ga!"

Is 5'5" and 125 lbs. (Can fit in your jeans.) Has never been in a fight.

Instagrams photos of sneakers with #risengrind #weouthere #WIP #yourMCM.

Complex and aspirational relationship with blackness.

Still won't let black people into his club.

"Dating" him means listening to him talk about vapes and saying the n-word. (You're not really dating him. You're "chilling with him sometimes" at his "crib.")

Genus: Hypebeast
Markings: Streetwear, knockoff Yeezys
Sounds: "If they can say it, why can't I?"

7) The Boy Who Desperately Wants to Be White

Has a picture of him holding two white girls on Tinder. The pic is six years old.

Refuses to watch Bollywood movies on principle. (*Loves* Wes Anderson movies.)

Went to college abroad. Every other sentence is about this experience.

Regularly submits essays to BuzzFeed and ScoopWhoop on interracial love and why it's revolutionary that he's dating Pamela.

Loves indie bands.

Was in an indie band in college.

He described the band as the desi Kings of Leon, the desi Mumford and Sons, the desi Bon Iver, or the desi The National. (He plays a tape for you. You hate it.)

Dating him means realizing that he's not over his (white) ex-girlfriend.

Genus: Hipster
Markings: Can be identified by his vape
Sounds: "It's not that I *prefer* white girls. It's just that I've never dated any Indian girls."

Drama Ranis: Field Notes

Father *to my mother*: Remember that time you lay down on the road because you were mad at me?

Me: Wait, wait, what?

Mother: Nothing.

Me: On the road?

Father: Mm-hm. She was annoyed at me for something—I don't remember what—and so she marched outside and lay on the main road.

Me, *snickering*: On the *road*?

Mother: Hmm, well, that was a long time ago. Anyway. What do you want for dinner?

Father: Luckily, there were no cars on the road at that time of the night. Or your mother would have been squished flat as a pancake in her quest to make a point.

Me: Wow.

Father: I know!

Mother: MOVING ON . . .

Father, *laughing heartily*: Can you imagine? Oh, your mother was a real drama queen.

* * *

"Brown girls are too much drama, mayne, that's why I like white girls." So goes the refrain of the desi fuckboy. You know the one: he's got a (six-year-old) picture of himself awkwardly clutching two white girls as his Tinder display picture.[1] When you press him on the issue, he says, "Look, I don't like arguing and I don't like drama. Indian girls take everything so seriously."

Leaving aside the sexism of that claim (I have never met a girl who was more dramatic than the men I have known), I want to address the underlying hypothesis. *Are* brown girls dramatic? Is this some sort of kink in our collective character? Is there even a driblet of truth to this accusation?

Brown *mums* are dramatic. This much we know. Brown mothers are always compensating late in life for their frustrated thespian dreams—overacting in word and gesture. They sigh heavily as they slap piping hot chapatis on to your plate. They go "uffo!" as they sink into welcoming sofas at the end of the day. They look heavenward and invoke every god in the Hindu pantheon when you disappoint them. One hand eternally on the hip, the other darting out like a snake to point out some dereliction of duty on the part of their children.

What is most terrifying about brown mothers is that you can't tell if they're upset right away. Their faces are emotionless, their tone of voice restrained at first. The drama takes a hot minute to get started.

White mums are direct. "No, you can't do that, Sandra. You're grounded." They play by Queensberry Rules. Brown mums? They hit well below the belt, everything is fair game—and they are prone to slip lead in the glove before the fight. Brown mums are *nasty*.

Any Conversation with a Brown Mum

You: Ma, can I go to Karan's house after I finish studying?

BM (Brown Mum), *setting down the plate she's washing, speaking in a deceptively calm voice*: Of course, you can, beta.

You, *not realizing the conversation isn't over*: Okay, I'm go—

BM: Why don't you stay there for the night too?

You, *confused by this escalation*: What?

BM, *speaking dangerously slowly*: Why not stay at Karan's house for the night too? Karan who? I never heard of this Karan before.

You: But I—

BM: Move in there. After all, you have so many friends to stay with. Karan, it seems. Karan who? Does he have a sister?

You: . . .

BM: Always wanting to go out. Is this a hotel? Why even live in the house? Why not just live outside? HAI RABBA!!!!

You, *making the mistake of laughing*: But, Ma—

BM: *Haanh*, laugh. It is all a joke to you. I'm ONLY put on this earth to give you permission to go out. Even though we are the ones who have provided this home for you. That doesn't matter to you. No, no, beta, Mama understands. Please go. *Jao*.

You: Oh my God—

BM, *sinking dramatically into a chair*: Let me die now, God. So that I no longer have to feel like a burden who is keeping you from doing the things you want to do. That is the only thing I have left to pray for. Shall I just die? Isn't that what you want?[2]

You: OK, OK, OK, fine, wow, I'm not going out. I'll just stay at home tonight.

BM, *instantly resumes her normal demeanour*: Accha, you want roti or rice for dinner?

If it is true that we all become our mothers, then it is the fate of every brown girl to become a drama-llama. But when does it start, this need to gesticulate wildly? To announce that "we want to die now" at the slightest inconvenience?[3]

Perhaps, it has something to do with the fact that the first TV show I ever watched was a soap opera. *The Bold and the Beautiful* was one of the only English shows that aired on Star World—at the all-important hour of 4–4.30 P.M. That was exactly when I got home from school, kicked off my shoes and socks, and sat in front of the TV with my "afternoon snack." (Milky tea and a couple of Bourbon biscuits, if I was lucky.)

The Bold and the Beautiful, for those of you not familiar with it, is a classic American soap opera. It follows the lives and loves of a fashion house in Los Angeles—Forrester. Replete with bottle-dye blondes, Botoxed bitchiness, and brittle plotlines, it was the most compelling thing I had ever seen. I watched (oftentimes open-mouthed) as pneumatic women wearing black lace seduced men with granite jaws. The men had improbable names like Ridge and Thorne. All of it seemed a million miles away from my demure existence in a sleepy south Indian town.

More than the sex, I loved the drama in it. I loved the fact that it took eight episodes to unravel the most basic plotline (who stole Eric Forrester's latest gown design?). Some mysteries (was Rick really C.J.'s illegitimate son?) took years. People died and came back to life, fashion empires rose and fell, hundreds of star-crossed young lovers eloped, and every single episode featured an intense close-up of a smouldering look. Nothing was minor in the world of *B&B*—it was drama on crack.

I understood that, though, in a way that I think many Americans could not. Nothing was minor in my world, either. Parents sobbed and created epic dramas over the tiniest of incidents: a lost pen, a ninety-seven on 100 (as opposed to a ninety-nine). A boy hugging a girl on school grounds was enough to create mass hysteria.[4] It was a culture of overreaction. If *The Bold and the Beautiful* set a certain standard for soapishness, our desi fare exceeded it easily.

One episode of *Sasural Simar Ka*[5] had this enchanting description:

> In tonight's episode, we will see Roli return after taking the spoon from Simar. But she bumps into Jhanvi and the spoon falls into muck. Will Jhanvi notice the spoon?

This was the burning question that would take twenty-five minutes to answer. I challenge anyone to read that description and not long to watch the show immediately.

Our movies were equally histrionic. Making my way through the Bollywood canon that I'd ignored as a teen, I noticed that we had certain uniquely Indian gestures.

A Short (but Not Exhaustive) Compendium of Bollywood Dramatic Gestures

1) *Hands folded in prayer (usually while kneeling before an elder)*

Perhaps the most iconic of all, this gesture was used to denote everything, from praying to "I beg you, the father of my bitterest enemy, to grant leave for your daughter to marry me." It is also used to beg for forgiveness (paired with the classic "Papa, *mujhe maaf karo*").

2) *One hand crumpled into a fist on the forehead, the other flung out behind you*

This gesture signifies calamity and despair. Perhaps, you have lost your ancestral lands to the evil moneylender whom you borrowed money from at 38 percent. Or maybe you are bemoaning the fact that your only daughter has betrayed you to marry the son of your bitterest enemy. In either case, this posture says, "Leave me, I want to be alone. I have nothing left in this duniya."

3) *Sobbing while lying sprawled on an exquisite divan while heartbreaking music swells*

For the full effect, the person who is sobbing on a divan must be wearing a voluminous, brilliantly colored lehenga (such as the ones worn in *Devdas*). The sobber usually lies face down on the divan but is arranged artfully so as to permit the viewer to see her trails of mascara.

4) *One hand extended in front of you, palm outward, as you stand in the courtyard of the zamindar's house*

To be done while delivering a coup de grace, such as: "*Yeh shaadi nahi ho sakti!*" This is a gesture of ineffable power, and as such can only be used *once* during the movie.

5) *Vampily smoking a cigarette*

Although cigarette smoking happens all over the world, vampy cigarette smoking only occurs in Bollywood movies of a certain kind. The kind of movie that features a "bad girl" wearing flimsy black blouses, doing item numbers in bars, and attempting to seduce every man, woman, and plant that comes her way.

Although Hollywood movies have their moments (somebody speeding to the airport to declare their love, deathbed confessions), they pale in comparison to ours.[6] The one Hollywood movie that I saw approaching desi levels of histrionics was *Moulin Rouge!* When I Googled it, I was unsurprised to find that Baz Luhrmann had been inspired by Bollywood.

"I watched a Hindi movie in Rajasthan," he explained in an interview about the film. "I loved it—it didn't seem to belong to any genre. The audience went from laughter to tears to being rapt at a love scene—I wanted to make a Hollywood movie that did the same." He was correct about Bollywood movies transcending genre—the only genre that we know is D-R-A-M-A.

But since ordinary brown women do not all have a Yash Raj staircase to sweep down, where does the drama manifest in our lives? I thought of the time I'd witnessed a furious outburst in a small Jaipur shop—a woman had figured out that the jewelery her husband had given her was fake. That! That was surely the kind of thing that was dramatic. The woman had caused a proper scene, so much so that I'd had to duck behind a counter to hide. (Only the wizened jeweler remained unmoved, and that was surely because he had seen a million similar dramas playing out.)

I composed a list of things that could reasonably lead a person to be dubbed "dramatic."

1) Storming out of an event
2) Faking your own death
3) Throwing a tantrum/having an argument somewhere public, like a grocery store
4) Making a playlist for your boyfriend and then *actually giving it to them*
5) Threatening to kill someone
6) Wearing a robe/gown/any material that sweeps the floor when you walk
7) Announcing that you are ready to die

To my horror, I scored four out of a possible seven. I'd stormed out of events, certainly. As a child, I'd thrown any number of tantrums (I quite enjoyed lying on the floor and beating my tiny wrists against it while my parents tried to calm me down). I owned a number of dramatic floor-sweeping gowns (who did I think I was? Scarlett O'Hara?) And yes, I recalled one particularly cold night in Boston when—after being unable to find a cab for hours—I had sat down on the pavement and told my friends to go on without me.

"I feel like Jack in *Titanic*," I said to them with a sigh. "I'll just sit here and wait for the cold to claim me." (They rolled their eyes and reminded me that I was about a twelve-minute walk from my house. Ten, if I walked briskly.)

I hadn't threatened to kill anyone—yet. Love had not driven me to do that most terrible of acts, making a playlist for my boyfriend. And I hadn't faked my own death.[7] But with such a high score on the Drama Scale, I couldn't call myself *un*dramatic. Ever since the age of nine, when I'd rushed down a mountain without talking to anyone, I'd been a Dramatic Debbie.[8]

Even with the books I read. I'd never much liked Jane Austen. I appreciated her genius, of course. Austen had nothing less than genius and any man who didn't admit that was surely being sexist. She was a brilliant satirist—but as a romance novelist? I'd always found her a little pallid. A little chilly for my tastes. There was precious little that was swoon-worthy in her work, which is why movie adaptations had to sex up the source material.

"My dear," brayed the men in her books, "I must declare that I have much regard for you and not a little care." At their most ardent, these men still resembled ice-cold turnips. Even Elizabeth Bennet—the maverick, the rebel—admitted that she only began loving Darcy after seeing his enormous house at Pemberley. I was not so sure that it was meant to be read as a joke. Elizabeth was not as impractical as people believed she was. The thought of Darcy's net worth—more than one—is likely to have flitted through her mind as she walked those English hills wordlessly. I pooh-poohed her notion of love—it felt more to me like two people liking each other and finding it convenient to get married.

No, I thought, the only satisfactory Austen heroine was Marianne Dashwood. Marianne was so dramatic that not only did she write impassioned love letters to her boyfriend, but she actually came down with a life-threatening fever when he didn't reply. I found that enormously satisfying, but, of course, Austen would not let her girl remain so dramatic. By the end of *Sense and Sensibility*, Marianne was a sober, dull creature, and was subjected to the cruel fate of marriage with a literal uncle. Like Mark Twain, I quite longed to dig Austen up and beat her over the skull with her own shinbone. I concurred with Charlotte Brontë that "the passions were perfectly unknown to her." An hour spent with Jane Eyre raging and storming around Thornfield was vastly preferable to me than an hour spent rearranging teacups with the Bennets.

In real life too. I rejected the notion that chill people were the most desirable friends. People who were like me—more quickly moved to anger—were also the more forgiving ones. It was the "chill" ones—the people who never said extravagant things while angry—who were the most grudging.

Poor things! Whenever I saw a drama-deficient person, I secretly wondered what outlet they had for their emotions. Whatever you threw at them, whatever difficult situations they went through, they remained quiet and restrained. They could never know the joys of surrendering oneself to the dramatic urge as I had when I had stood on a railway platform and thought to myself that I was *just like Anna Karenina.*

They could not understand why I'd wanted to be a trial lawyer in the first place—what the inescapable lure was about the polished gleam of a courtroom, or how tremendously fulfilling it was to get up and say, "Elias for the Commonwealth," or to thunder, "Objection, Your Honor! Commonwealth is badgering my witness!" There was a luxuriance in drama, a spreading out, a kind of generosity of spirit that the rational could never know, I thought. People who don't have a flair for the dramatic cannot understand the appeal of a heel exit turn, of the pleasures of angrily snipping ex-boyfriends out of family photos, or the urge to sob on a decadent couch. They will grow up to be parents who do not sit quietly in the dark with the light switched off.[9]

I contemplate their deprivations as I apply my lipstick (a shade fittingly called "Red Drama"). The fashion magazines have told me that I can't do a bold eye *and* a bold lip together. "It's too much." Just to prove them wrong, I add an extra layer of kajal to my waterline. Women who wear dramatic makeup are not to be trifled with, we all know from film noir. And I am a dramatic woman. That's okay.

The thing about being dramatic is this: it often means "a woman who's not afraid to make a fuss." Dramatic women aren't docile, you see. Dramatic women are loud, messy, passionate, and colorful. They are remembered long after they exit the room in a furious whirl of draperies. And dramatic women aren't the same as toxic women, or abusive women, or bitchy women. Dramatic women rarely hurt people with our excesses. We only want to be heard.

Yes, my mother is a drama rani. If I ever have daughters, I think they'd be dramatic too. It's in our blood—singing hot and loud—and you know what? I like it. I fucking love it. May our shadows never diminish. May every door we slam resound loudly and every incandescent emotion that we express be appreciated.

IV
HURT

If Your Heart Is Broken, Read This

A long time ago, I read a paper on zebrafish. The abstract explained that any kind of cardiac injury in mammals and amphibians is permanent and typically leads to scarring. But the zebrafish—a small, silvery, commonplace-looking fish—has the ability to regenerate its heart. If its heart is severely damaged, it can simply grow fresh cardiac muscle to replace what is lost. It is called heart regeneration and is unheard of in any other species.

For a few days, I was obsessed with this information. I looked up everything I could find on aberrant or strangely built hearts. I found strange tidbits of information that I still remember. Jellyfish, for instance, have three hearts. I dreamed of jellyfish, iridescent ribbons floating in a tank, and their internal organs wrapped around each other.

Did you know wood frogs can stop their hearts when they're frozen? They basically put them on ice for the duration of the long winter. For some time, I dreamed of wood frogs too, caught in the middle of a lolloping-away, petrified in a pond-chamber of ice.

I don't know what I was looking for. Perhaps I was thinking about the operation that someone in my family had recently undergone. It was an open-heart surgery, my uncle told me. I knew nothing about medicine and all that this conveyed to me was the opposite: closed-heart surgery. There was something particularly vulnerable about a scalpel going into an open heart, I thought. The one time my uncle took me to a hospital (to show me what an operating room looked like), I whimpered and turned away from the glass. My only memory is of a spreading redness.

There are many things that can go wrong with a heart: arrhythmia, cardiac arrest, a murmur. Some of these sound vaguely and impossibly romantic. I wondered what could go wrong with my own heart and when that would happen.

Here is a story for you. I was not an attractive child. Or—more accurately—I was an attractive child who became an unattractive teenager. I wore soft-pink glasses that made me look more owl-like than most owls do. The rest of my face refused to catch up to my nose, and my hips were starting to thicken to a sluggish fat. Above all, I was dull and shy. There was no vivacity or quickness in my movements, and I was never one of the names scrawled passionately into a school desk with a pencil. I didn't mind. Much. I accepted this as the natural order of things. I'd never been an overly dramatic girl.

However, there was a boy. One boy. When he stood up from his desk, I noticed. I noticed the way he stood in the morning assembly and looked for his face in any crowd. When he played cricket on the school grounds, when he ran in his clean whites on Sports Day, when he walked down the corridors with his prefect's badge on, I felt something. A minor tremor. It would have been classified as minor, but it was *there*, and it meant something to my twelve-year-old heart.

Of course, I never dreamed anything would come of it. I knew—even then—that he was in some upper echelon of coolness that I could never hope to access, awkward as I was. It was enough for me to look at him sometimes in class; he never even entered my daydreams.

When my best friend pressed me about my school crushes—
"Come on! Priya! You must have some"—I reluctantly admitted
that maybe, *he* was one. A few days later, I found a letter in my
school bag.

It was elaborately illustrated, came in a pink-'n'-glitter
envelope. This, of course, should have warned me. A thirteen-
year-old boy would not, *could not*, use such an envelope. And the
letter was still more improbable, declaring as it did his violent
crush on me. At the bottom was his signature, in a large, confident
hand—the prefect's.

I weighed it in my hand and shook it as if it could crumble to
pink dust. I ran to my best friend and informed her of the miracle.

He likes you! she said. She did not seem surprised at all (another
clue). I asked her what I ought to do about it.

"It says he's too shy to talk about this," I told her. He wasn't at
all. The boy I knew was jaunty. I had a hard time believing that he
meant it. "But I want to ask him about it indirectly."

He was right there in the classroom. It was lunch break
and kids were eating Parle-G biscuits and undoing their tightly
knotted ties. I walked towards him—what unearthly confidence
possessed me, I do not know—and asked him whether he'd left
anything in my school bag.

The answer came quickly. Immediately. *No.* Not a "no" of
shame, but one of surprise. He looked astonished at the very
question, which was what led me to understand. He wasn't lying.
He hadn't left it in my bag.

I can summon to this very day the expression on his face, so
clearly, so perfectly. So it must have been a significant event in
my young life. I wondered what moved my best friend to write
that letter, to pretend it was from him. Was it a gesture of cruelty
or one of misplaced kindness? I would never know, but what it
produced in me was not kindness. But maybe something like
heartbreak.

Theory

More people die of heartbreak than of radiation, says Saul Bellow. At first, I couldn't believe it. It sounded impossibly melodramatic: an ailment particular to the Victorian period. It is what happens to the virtuous Madame de Tourvel in *Les Liaisons Dangereuses*. After having been seduced by the novel's wicked protagonist, she is cruelly rebuffed and her grief is so absolute that she succumbs to it. She dies of heartbreak.

And yet. Death from heartbreak is not unknown to medicine. The death of a long-time partner affects the risk of atrial fibrillation—a form of arrhythmia in which the upper chambers of the heart beat irregularly, reducing blood flow to the rest of the body. Studies have shown that the chance of heart attacks rises drastically in the year after one's spouse dies. The lagging mechanisms of the body—perhaps this was its way of shutting shop. Nothing more to see here, it declares. The will to live is gone, gone with the beloved. Just as boy band JLS sang in their breakout hit:

> We should've stayed together
> 'Cause when you left me it stopped
> They're telling me
> My heart won't beat again
> Won't beat again

There is a ridiculous extravagance to the metaphor that is appealing. How else do you describe that pain? When doctors ask you to describe the quality of the pain—is heartbreak more of a sharp, bright pain or a dull ache? Is it constant or flickering? Does it stab or is it superficial? There was a boy who reportedly stabbed himself with a geometry compass, or maybe it was a protractor (rumors vary) because Susan in Class VIII rejected his proposal. When asked, he said he was trying to carve her name into him. It made a twisted kind of sense; it was the only time she would leave her mark on his skin.

It happens.

Another woman—a friend of the family—rolled around on the floor crying hysterically when her heart had been broken. I heard of the event but found my imagination failing as I tried to picture it. A fifty-something woman reduced to such a state over love was incomprehensible to me. Although, of course, it happens.

In college, a friend of mine gave me her phone on a Saturday night. Her instructions were explicit: I was not to let her have it when she got drunk, no matter how much she begged me. She was getting over a boy, and she didn't want to crack and call him. *I promise*, I said. *I promise I won't let you have it.*

Only two hours later, she was running down the street after me, screaming that she needed it back. Her eyelashes were stiff and spiky with tears, and her accent thickened by alcohol.

"Please," she said. "I *need* to call him. I *have* to call him."

I stood there for a moment, wondering what to do. I thought of all the times she'd called him previously and how careless he had been. How he even refused to pick up sometimes. If I gave her the phone, would it do any good? He was a boy who never thought of her. I would only be ensuring a repeat of her current performance.

"I lost it," I told her. "I don't know where it is. It's somewhere at home, maybe. Forget about it. You can't make any calls tonight."

When she finally understood what I was saying—that there was no room for negotiation—all the anger went out of her like air. She slumped down to the pavement, like a balloon that had been pricked. Slack with sorrow.

People stopped to look at her. Even among the drunk revelers on the street, she stood out. Her sadness was so large, you couldn't ignore it. I suddenly noticed that she was only wearing one shoe.

"Where's your other shoe?"

She gazed vacantly downward and shrugged. It didn't matter to her. And in her indifference, I saw that this was heartbreak: a state in which you didn't care if you were only wearing one shoe.

It happens.

What to do about our hearts?

I saw a music video once in which a girl carries a heart. It is her own heart, huge and shining. It is so large that it doesn't fit into cabs. It is so large that doormen at restaurants don't let her in. It is so large that everybody avoids her. Nobody wants to see a human heart so nakedly. A heart is a pulsating, terrible thing. Like the madman in Edgar Allen Poe's *The Tell-Tale Heart*, we wish to bury it under the floorboards. We hope that will muffle its desperate beating. And that is only for a heart that is whole. What can we do about a heart that is broken?

Girls begin to message me, lots of girls (sometimes boys too, though not often): what do we do with our broken hearts? when will they heal? is there some perfect combination of steps that will ensure healing? cutting him off, moving houses, sleeping with other people, drinking a lot, not drinking at all, what will finally do it? *something* must do it? Hearts have to heal, won't they?

Underneath, there is a note of panic. Can a heart not heal?

In *Great Expectations*, Miss Havisham tells Pip frenziedly: "Love her, love her, love her! If she favours you, love her. If she wounds you, love her. If she tears your heart to pieces—and as it gets older and stronger, it will tear deeper—love her, love her, love her!" I imagine Pip's heart before me, as vivid as a cow's heart on the biology lab table. (I saw one once. It was so large I wanted to cry.) I picture Pip's heart rolling downhill, like a tire, gathering pieces of glass, metal, and other things that would hurt it. Absorbing them into its soft tissue. Growing bigger and stronger so that the glass would cut more. A heart with a mutated core.

"There are many ways of breaking a heart. Stories were full of hearts broken by love, but what really broke a heart was taking away its dream—whatever that dream might be," said Pearl S. Buck. Perhaps that is true. But what is certainly true is that I have seen many hearts broken for and by love.

I read *Brighton Rock* one summer on my dad's recommendation. My dad is very literary but his taste tends towards the dry. Saul Bellow, Kingsley Amis (at whom I roll my eyes—I can't stand that old misogynist). He likes the kind of books in which nothing happens for eighty pages, and then someone commits adultery and the sky turns grey. I cannot abide that kind of book.

But I have *Brighton Rock* on my iPad, so I start reading it. To my astonishment, Graham Greene is nothing like I expected. He writes like a forest fire. Exciting, impossible things happen: gangsters choke each other with candy; lovers are knifed and cars crash; and a good girl falls in love with a bad boy (I am amused by this most Bollywood of touches). Her name is Rose and she is a barmaid who loves Pinkie (not an improbable name to us desis) with all the desperation of a first love. She gives up her job, her life, her family, everything, to tie her fortunes to a skinny murderer and gang leader.

He does not love her—does not care tuppence about her—but he must marry her because she was a witness to his crimes. When he comes to a bad end, as he must (Greene is as annoyingly moralistic as any Sanjay Leela Bhansali film), we, the readers, are relieved: now Rose will never know that her husband did not love her. But, alas! Pinkie had made a record on his honeymoon, stating what he really thought of her and his absolute contempt for his wife of only one day. She, poor thing, goes home to listen to it after his death, under the impression that it is a declaration of his love. It is the only record of him he has left.

Rose's waiting fate—a heartbreak so absolute that it happens off the page—is described by Greene as "the worst horror of all." It is like the scene in *Oedipus Rex* where Oedipus stabs his eyes with his mother's brooch. Such things, Sophocles seems to say, ought not to be witnessed. Pinkie has died, that was inevitable. But what of Rose's heart? What will be left of her *life*?

Blondie sings, "Once I had a love and it was a gas/soon turned out had a heart of glass." (The original line was something else, but I could see why they chose that image: there is something arresting about it. It is as sharp as . . . well, glass.) Bonnie Tyler sings "Total Eclipse of the Heart" as if the heart could fall into shadow. And Toni Braxton—oh, Toni!—wails in glorious, all-saturating melancholy in "Unbreak My Heart." The listener knows the song title is a lie: there will be no un-breaking of this particular heart. The woman who waits for her man to come back will never see him walk through the door again, of that we are sure. Sorrow is absolute and without the possibility of mitigation.

The writer in me appreciates the finality of this devastation. Anything else would be anticlimactic. The man cannot walk back through the door. If a glass heart shattered, it could never be put back together. And yet, is there not some part of you that wants to reach through the bars of the song and console the singer? Who, on reading *Romeo and Juliet*, has not been tempted to tell young Juliet (not yet thirteen! What troubled you at thirteen that you didn't immediately forget?) that she will heal, that life will go on. That it may seem impossible, but it does. Because it must.

People often ask me what to do about their broken hearts. They ask me for advice, which I give sparingly (advice, as the poets have said, is a dangerous business). I give them soft, clean words of sympathy. Think about it. What would you want to do? Do not despair. Life goes on. Time heals all. Clichés.

I can feel their scorn at my humble offerings. They want different advice, so does everybody. Nobody who writes to "Ask

Polly" is happy with what they hear. They are looking for radical advice and they think that because I do not have it, I have not yet had my heart broken. But no, like everyone else, I have had a heartbreak that cleaned my clock. Everyone seems to have had one. Somebody who ruined them for everybody else. Mine came late, at twenty-eight. That's the only difference.

In order to understand this part, you have to understand one thing about me: I wasn't really loved before this boy. Oh, I'd had boyfriends, of course. I'd dated a big, confident white boy in law school, for instance. Let's call him J. *He* didn't love me.

Looking back, I am not even sure that J liked me. What I did know was that he was intensely attracted to me and maybe he mistook that for likeness. He didn't ever talk about how he felt about me, other than saying that he thought I was beautiful.

I wasn't sure if he had feelings in the way other people had feelings. He had a sociopathic quality to him. (Or, perhaps, I imagined this because it is softer on my ego.)

"I guess I should pick you up at the station," he said when I visited him in Washington. I'd been on the bus for eight hours or so. I'd gotten on the bus at Boston. Four hours to New York. Another four to D.C. And thirty dollars (a lot to a broke law student).

He lived less than an hour from the train station but he couldn't be bothered to come pick me up.

"Isn't that what people do? Pick up their girlfriends from the bus station?" he had said.

"You don't have to do that," I had said. "I'm fine." I hadn't thought about it before but it occurred to me that if the positions were reversed, I would have picked him up from the station. I would have been thrilled to do it. I wouldn't have even asked; I would have done it instinctively.

I wasn't really used to being loved. All I'd had was a handful of flings with uncaring men and abortive OkCupid dates. I hadn't yet read Warsan Shire: "how far have you walked for men who've never held your feet in their laps?" I didn't know that love meant going to the bus station. How strange it is the fact that you need to get used to being loved.

I watch shows about heartbreak though. On *Ally McBeal*, the protagonist meets her ex-boyfriend (her big love, Billy, the boy next door) and asks if he's single. When he tells her *no*, he's married now, she simply says, *oh*. Billy doesn't see it, but the audience is granted a visual of a bouquet of arrows flying into her chest. She has been stricken, and only we know this.

Heartbreak is rarely confined to one moment. When you look back on it, you don't have the luxury of a neat tracking shot a la Ally. *This moment. That was when my heart broke.* Instead, we have what seems like endlessness. A new desolation that we step into, like Leonardo DiCaprio on his knees, sobbing, when he hears that his beloved, Juliet, has died. "Then I defy you, stars!" He has entered into a new world, one in which it doesn't matter much what he does or what the result is.

My mother reminds me of her friend, the fifty-something woman who fell in love. When her heart was finally broken by the man she was in love with, she rolled around on the floor crying. Nobody could stop her, my mother says. "She just rolled around and around on the dusty floor, weeping." I wonder at that: that self-indulgent manifestation of grief. I wonder how it feels. I have never been in love, so I can only guess.

Practice

The one that changed all that—the boy who broke my heart— came much later, when I was twenty-seven and had grown comfortable with my singleness. Perhaps, I was too comfortable. Perhaps, I was complacent.

In *The God of Small Things*, Arundhati Roy writes of what happens when Margaret meets a man named Chacko: "Margaret Kochamma's tiny, ordered life relinquished itself to this truly baroque bedlam with the quiet gasp of a warm body entering a chilly sea." It was a little like that.

Part of it was that he lived (like Chacko did) like a "messy, exiled prince." He was so different from the boys I'd met in Delhi with their carefully shellacked hair and personalities. When I think of him, I think of ash on my sheets, the singe of a duvet where he'd dropped a joint; a coffee stain (he drank coffee constantly, preferring it to food most days); his small pile of books; headphones, other boyish toys. He was a mess. It was, I confess, exhilarating at first. The craziness of it. For he was crazy. He told me so right away in a singsong voice. "I don't mean crazy in the way that men say crazy, baby, I mean crazy!!!!!!"

We'd met outside a bar on a summer night. I noticed things about him, his burnished body—the place where his collarbones rose out of his T-shirt. He had the hips of a boy. I felt a jolt of instant lust, the kind of lust that women keep secret from men because it borders on the vulgar. When he asked for my number, I gave it to him, never imagining he would call.

On our first date, he drank my whiskey. He didn't ask permission, he just took it.

I ought to have been annoyed but I wasn't particularly. The fact that we had shared the whiskey made everything comfortable. It had created a sudden intimacy between us, breaking up the normal awkwardness of a first date. I felt as if I was sitting with my brother or perhaps an annoying cousin, and that we would shortly get up and go to dinner, squabbling. I didn't realize then that that was his way with everybody. That he asked for things so gorgeously, so sweetly, that you liked him better than somebody who asked for nothing.

We spent the next three days in my bed, mostly sleeping and watching bad television shows. He rolled joint after joint, so many that I felt woozy off the fumes. My sheets were burnt and black with ash, but changing them didn't seem important. We ordered takeout—cauliflower in gluey soup, chicken dyed an orange-cone color—and ate it while it was still hot enough to make us sweat. We spent the rest of the summer together.

There were warning signs, of course. He told me about his episodes, how he punched the wall until his fists came away bloody, how he felt as if nobody would be quiet inside his mind, "all the clichés." The medication made him fuzzy so he stopped taking it. He said there were voices inside his head, minor demons. He asked if I was scared of him.

"No." This time I was lying.

"It's okay if you are," he said, looking at me seriously. I saw that his beauty had a sharpness to it: everything in his face was sharp and tight, as if it had been sculpted by somebody who had no material to spare. "I love you."

It was the first time someone had said that to me. It is a stunning moment, the first time somebody tells you that they love you when there's nothing to coax it forward—not liquor or drugs or even the intimacy of sunsets. "Ah," cries the soul, freewheeling over the plain, "I am loved!"

This was the first man I knew who liked to hold somebody all night long. In bed, his body was warm, like a small animal's. I felt the bones of his back; he pressed against my chilly skin and refused to let go. When I got up to go to the bathroom, he flailed, thrashing his body about the bed until he found me again. I thought of my other boyfriends, those who'd let me sleep on my side of the bed after a quick hug goodnight. Two people could not sleep so closely without a certain discomfort. And yet he did—he slept evenly, serenely through the night, clutching my breast. It was, I thought, because there was no embarrassment or self-consciousness in his love. He had not learnt the language of restraint, of emotion denied. He called me his wife in front of strangers, kissed me at the cinema, wrote me songs as desperate as himself. I was frightened by such intensity. It was like a room, I thought, that was bigger from the inside than it seemed from the outside. If you had asked me before, *what is love?* I would have given a different answer.

His mind was always rattling in his skull, like a mouse inside a clock, giving him no peace. He picked fights with strangers to quieten it.

"I want to fight with that man," he said, pointing to a stranger in a blue hat. "And that one. But not that one."

"Why?"

"He's soft inside," he said. "You shouldn't damage people like that, only the ones who can take it."

That summed up, in a funny way, his attitude towards the world. He was a child himself, but he understood some things about sensitivity. There was a rage inside him at odds with that sensitivity and it leaked out in driblets and sometimes in a gush. When we argued—which we did with startling violence—I believe he felt worse about his words than I did. He said unforgivable things, abusive things, hateful things in his rages. I told myself it was the price I had to pay for him being tender for the rest of the time.

At least we always made up afterwards, I told myself. He crawled back into bed, like an ashamed puppy, his nose soft and quivering, begging for forgiveness.

I always forgave him. Late at night, when he was asleep, I'd watch Tamil songs that he could translate for me.

Enadhu selvam nee/
izaithu kavita nee/ezuthup pizhaiyum nee/
iraval velicham nee/iravin kaneer nee/
enadhu vaanam nee/izandhu siragum nee/
naan thooki valarthu nee

I could make out a few fragments of meaning here and there.

You are my wealth and also my poverty. You are my poem but also the flaw in my writing.

Even now, when I get to the line, "You are the sorrow that I lovingly raised," I weep, for it is about him.

On *BoJack Horseman*—a show about a sad cartoon horse that has no right to be as profound as it is—a couple breaks up. *It's funny*, says Wanda, the owl, to her boyfriend, BoJack. "When you look at someone through rose-colored glasses, all the red flags just look like flags."

Wanda, *c'est moi.*

We went on like that—on and on—for two years. It was torture and it hollowed me out from the inside to love somebody—so much!—who was not unqualifiedly kind to me. Even now I can say little of it; it pains me too much to write about the bad parts.

The ring of broken whiskey glasses. The sound of him fighting with people. The sound of fists. The sound of a slap ringing in the darkness. Sad songs in the night, his voice holding a note as beautiful as any the Weeknd might have sung.

The tears, so many tears. So little that is banal or ordinary to most couples, because *he* is hurting. And his hurt is so large that it looms so magnificently that I have no space to feel my own hurt. I am the shock absorber to his shock. The cotton wrapping to his hard edges. He tells me that I have had an easy life compared to his. I have had a soft life. I am fattened on privilege. *My* parents never held my hands over an open flame to punish me because I took ten rupees from their purse. *My* parents never hit or verbally abused me. *I* am not the one who has demons whispering in her ear, "Kill yourself! Kill yourself!"

All of this is undeniable. And yet, something about this equation seems cruel. Because I have had a soft life, must I eat the bullets he feeds me regularly? For—despite the glory of that magical world that we have built together—my body is full of bullets.

"*Bang bang, he shot me down, bang bang, I hit the ground, bang bang . . .*"

I know I cannot go on like this. When the break comes, it is inevitable, and I am the one to do it.

"I think we shouldn't see each other any more."

I don't do anything I'm not supposed to. I don't call when he asks me not to. I don't show up outside his house. My sorrow is expressed only to myself. (Women know all about that.)

So many times a day I want to write his name. I check his "last seen" on WhatsApp to see if he's blocked me yet. It is a dreary ritual, but as necessary to me as air.

The only way I have ever known to get over things is by reading. In reading, I feel my own miseries dissolve and take on the shape of someone else's.

I pull out and reread old books I loved. My favorite ones. *Jane Eyre*, the first grown-up book that I loved. In it, Charlotte Brontë created the portrait of a man who loved Jane ardently, unselfishly, eternally—Edward Rochester. It was not something Brontë had known in real life. In real life, Brontë had fallen in love with a Belgian teacher she'd met at boarding school. A married teacher by the name of Constantin Héger.

Little is known of their interaction, but it is certain that Brontë was passionately attached to him. In January 1845, Brontë wrote to Héger:

> If my master withdraws his friendship from me entirely I shall be absolutely without hope—if he gives me a little friendship—a very little—I shall be content—happy, I would have a motive for living—for working. Monsieur, the poor do not need a great deal to live on—they ask only the crumbs of bread which fall from the rich men's table—but if they are refused these crumbs—they die of hunger—

Her letters are profoundly sad; they reveal how little Brontë asked. She did not expect him to love her, not even to have a whole friendship with her. All she asked for from Héger was a letter—a very occasional letter. This letter was the lynchpin on which her whole life turned; it was the only thing that gave her solace in her miserable life at Haworth.

> I am dimly aware that there are some cold and rational people who would say on reading [this] [. . .] —'she is raving'—My sole revenge is to wish these people—a single day of the torments that I have suffered for eight months— then we should see whether they wouldn't be raving too—

In *Villette*, Brontë wrote a heroine, Lucy Snowe, who was loved by a dark, saturnine professor (modeled after Héger). At the end of the book, Lucy marries her professor. But the real-life ending for Brontë was not destined to be such.

Brontë's last letter to her professor went unanswered. Alongside the last page is a hastily scribbled address of a cobbler. Héger had used her last, most anguished letter, as scrap paper.

In my own despair, I look for useful action. Like so many women before me, I turn to one of the few things I can exert absolute control over: my hair.

Oh, it looks above-board. I take out magazines, I browse Instagram accounts. I could color my hair, but it is expensive. I want to do something cheap and drastic, not acquire subtly blond highlights. What would be drastic for me? I watch *The Hunger Games* and admire Natalie Dormer's half-shaved blonde head. She looks so much stronger than me and filled with a tough, manly spirit. I want to look like that, I tell myself, and pretend it's an aesthetic choice.

I could go to a salon, but I decide to do it at home.

I don't even have proper clippers so I use scissors for the first half of it. I cut and cut my hair (currently at breast-length) until there are only small tufts sticking straight up.

I look in the mirror and stifle a giggle. I look like Sonic the Hedgehog. Then, I grow serious. Slowly (but not too carefully), I shave half my scalp with a razor. To the pink.

My scalp is covered in cuts but I've done it. Trembling, I get up from my crouching position. My hair, my beautiful hair has been thinned out thoroughly. Half lost. But I've done it; I look like something altogether unfamiliar. Something rich and strange.

I tell my friends I did it because I wanted a change, and they believe me. I say I wanted to be edgy. Switch my style up. I take photos of myself and post them on social media with the caption "half-monk, half-hitman." I pretend that this was a controlled decision and not the result of a break with sanity. I refuse to let myself remember Britney Spears in 2007, those images of her shaving her own head in the barbershop with a manic kind of glee. She must have been so desperate, Britney, when she was under a conservatorship and couldn't control her own affairs despite being the most powerful female entertainer in the world. She must have longed for a way to scream at the world: *Look, bitch! I'm here and I have control.*

Do I have control over myself? I tell myself that I do.

I get drunk—well, more drunk than usual—at the bar one night. When I'm in the loo, I hear a hammering of fists on the door. It's just a group of boys saying, "Hurry up!" Their bladders are full and their patience shortened by beer.

I stride out of the bathroom and look one in the eye. The cockiest, most aggressive-looking one.

"Do you want to fight?"

He is taken aback. I am standing very close to him. Too close. I could grab him by the collar now or practice the moves I learned in my mixed martial arts classes. A rear-naked choke. A guillotine choke. Or something less elaborate still. A clean right hook or jab to his smug chin.

"Let's go outside."

He's with three friends. Four men on one. I remember what my MMA instructor had taught me. If you're outnumbered, just run. You're basically fucked. It doesn't matter who you are, you can't fight and win under those circumstances.

I realize with a sense of relief that I want to be clobbered. It would, I think, be a new experience. I have no desire to win, which is why I want to fight. I don't mind lying bloody in the mud, tasting the salt in my mouth as my consciousness fades to black.

Truly, a broken heart makes teenagers of us all.

But that day, I didn't fight. The boys left quietly. Without making a fuss. Their faces resigned; perhaps, they realized I would cause much more trouble than they were prepared for.

* * *

In Anne Carson's poem "The Glass Essay," she describes the end of an affair, one of six years with a man she calls Law. "Perhaps the hardest thing about losing a lover is/to watch the year repeat its days," she writes, and I sob with her, because I know there was sobbing involved in the writing of the line. Perhaps not in the final iteration. The final iteration of the poem is, as the title would suggest, cold as glass. It is refined, polished like crystal; it holds a mirror up to heartbreak and tells us coolly, clearly, what that experience is like. But Anne Carson writes the truth and I can feel her heart throbbing in that poem. It is as if I could feel the tears that she dried—or perhaps the ones that she let fall unchecked—when she thought of that: "The hardest thing about losing a lover is/to watch the year repeat its days."

How does she cope with it? Oh, by sitting on the floor (not rolling, not Anne) and chanting bits of old Latin prayers. "*De profundis clamavi ad te Domine*" (Out of the depths of my soul, I cry to you, oh Lord).

I wonder if I can try it. There is a simplicity about it that pleases me. "Getting religion," as atheists put it.

Getting religion was what Peony did in the book by Pearl S. Buck. She fell in love with a man—a man she couldn't have because she was a servant and he was the master of the house. At the height of her love and desperation, she turns to the convent. She shaves her head and becomes a nun. Years later, when she is asked if her love has died, she *smiles* and says *no*. Her love has been diffused, she explains, she no longer loves one man but all. In that kind of love, there is no heartbreak, only beatitude.

It seems nice, I think. Perhaps I can access it too, that feeling of goodwill for all.

I sit on my roof in the dead of night, watching the stars twinkle and disappear briefly behind the polluted air. It is hard to breathe in Delhi this winter; we fall sick. Of course, I am not the ordinary kind of sick, I think to myself wryly. Or, am I? It is such a common kind of sickness that I have.

I stay up late every night, doing . . . not much of anything at all. When I look back at those nights, I'm not sure how to account for my activities. I drank, I know this. I drank cheap whiskey. The kind that Punjabi farmers pour into their trucks when they're out of diesel because it'll keep them going just a little longer. Under the stars, I pray for the same.

"I talk to God but the sky is empty," Sylvia Plath wrote in a letter to Richard Sassoon in 1950. I can imagine her—clever and lovely Sylvia—sitting atop another terrace, her face upturned to the sky. Another woman who knew all about heartbreak. She described the quality of her pain as an "owl's talons clenching my heart."

It really does feel like that. It is an extraordinary discovery, the discovery that heartbreak is a physical pain. It is lodged between the third and fourth ribs, and it aches in much the same way as an injured muscle. It is an injured muscle.

I go to visit one of my dearest friends who is suffering similarly. Lying on the couch in her Hauz Khas apartment, we toss back shots of whiskey (more expensive than the kind I usually drink).

"There's an Urdu poem," she tells me (half-laughing), "that goes, 'In heartbreak, it is actually the liver that suffers.' *Haina*?"

We laugh, but keep drinking.

Sometimes we go out, try to meet other men. This is not a romantic process; it's something we describe as hunting and gathering. We're looking for a stranger's dick, simple as that. It's one way to get over someone. Getting (as the ancients would put it) under somebody else.

I do not know how men handle heartbreak. I can guess though. Maybe they shrug it off and keep walking, pretending that they're not wounded. I have heard that when you are stabbed, you don't always feel it right away. You can walk down a street and collapse in the end. I think that maybe men do that. "How is it so easy for men to get over a three-year relationship?" somebody asks me. I think, maybe it is not easy. There are clues. Even in their stoicism, in their stillness, there are hints of pain—when they call you at 4 A.M., ten years after the relationship ended; the way they say, "She was the one that got away," about a high-school relationship.

I'm thinking of all the women I know who've suffered at the end of a relationship. How I've run to them, with a handle of whiskey and a carton of cherry ice cream. I've run to their houses at night, and we've discussed their feelings over and over. Taken apart the pain and looked at it unflinchingly. Everything that happened to us and how we feel about it.

Do men do the same? I think of an episode of *Friends* that I had watched long ago, in which Chandler is depressed about the end of a relationship. To cheer him up, his boys take him to a strip club.

Maybe all Miss Havisham needed was some girlfriends and to eat the wedding cake with champagne. Maybe if she'd had a group of mates who'd have laughed at her man and said, "You know, I always thought he had knobbly knees." Maybe she wouldn't have shuttered herself away from the world, drawn the curtains, and refused to change out of her wedding dress. At the very least, she would have learned this: that life goes on.

Doesn't it? That's what Cher sang on her breakout track, "Believe." I first heard that wonderfully husky voice when I was in school, at about twelve or thirteen years old.

"Do you believe in life after love?/I can feel something inside me saying, '*I really don't think you're strong enough.*'"

The words are positive, powerful—an anthem for girls everywhere but I am not sure I can trust Cher. Oh, not about life going on. I know life goes on. It seems to hurtle relentlessly forward—I am strapped in a seat on a train I do not want to be on. I still have to get up each morning and brush my teeth, eat my breakfast, show my face to my family. I have to continue to be, somehow.

My question is this: will life go on in the same way as it did before? Will I ever again look forward to things? (Investigate: after any distressing event, can life ever go on in the same way as it did before?)

I am a heartbroken writer who writes mostly about dating and relationships. The irony is not lost on me: the fact that I have none of the handy, pocket-size wisdom I usually dispense. It is impossible for me to write an easy explainer "How to Get over Someone" for Cosmopolitan.com. (3,500 words, fairly compensated.) They are not in me.

Irony #2, for the folks counting at home: I have always written the most about love when I have not been in love at all.

I pull up an old blog that I kept in law school. It is as bad as I had feared, like coming across a childish drawing of sunset over mountains when you are an adult. Every second poem is about love, which I imagine in a series of overwrought metaphors. I cut scraps out of each poem, methodically. I try to make them amount to something profound. Love is like squeezing the juice out of oranges with your bare hands.

I turn away, flinching from the sudden sprays and my eyes stinging while you lean against the cold countertop and say nothing when I tell you that the orange stopped running down the hill because it ran out of juice and the joke hangs there like a question and I'm left with the mess of rind and gut that I couldn't separate cleanly from the flesh. I scoop them into the waste sloppily, so that seeds drop into the rug that I can't get out so I catch my breath and draw the back of my hand across my forehead where it leaves wetness and then—this one thing I do properly—like you, I drop the knife into the sink and we both watch the plate in your silence as acidic as the oranges.

Love Is Like Mathematics

Kolmogorov's axioms of probability suggest that the probability of a coin landing on either heads or tails is one, but that the possibility of it landing on neither heads nor tails is zero. Either I would have met you, or I would never have met you. If I met you, I would have loved you. If I did not meet you, I would not have loved you. I find myself, contrary to all reasonableness, wishing for an outcome in which neither of these events occurred or did not occur. I postulate that the probability that I would be able to heal our relationship is unfeasibly small. In the event that I could heal our relationship, the probability that I would be able to reverse the inexorable progression of time is zero. And yet, I imagine myself defying logic, forever watching, suspended in time, your hair lit by the bar lamps until it appears to me like a corona. I imagine probability, against all the rules of probability, as a little demon, one whose life I extinguished long ago so that we could be together in every

iteration of the world, every what-if, every universe in which every
possible event that occurred was only me loving you.

* * *

Love is like watching the lights go out in a foggy park. Love is cruel
and kind, petty and glorious, it is at once (like Plácido Domingo sings)
a holding on, and a letting go.

* * *

Love is so short, but forgetting is so long.

* * *

This is it, this is your life. This is the gift of pain smoothed over; this
is the deepness; the strange spark; the pure burn of altars. This is
happiness. This is the forgetting of a face.

* * *

In all this mess of metaphor, have I found anything worthwhile to
say about love? What can I, who have had so much to say about
broken hearts, offer you now that will not be trite?

I tweeted once, "When you are heartbroken, start a new
Netflix show. Something that you have never watched with your
love. Do not binge: your heart has had enough of that. Watch one
episode a day. Feel the passage of time. Time is the kindest of all
things in this mysterious universe. With time, you will heal."

I examine my own words for their truth. Has my heart
healed? Not yet, but I want to believe it will. What I want is heart
regeneration. Like a zebrafish. For all of us, for the long dead and
buried women like Charlotte Brontë. (She died, I believe, with

her heart still broken.) For the living, for these girls who weep with contorted faces in club bathrooms, their mascara dripping on to the indifferent floor.

Zadie Smith, one of my favorite writers, presents the view in *White Teeth* that these girls are feeling entitled to love:

> It's a funny thing about the modern world. You hear girls in the toilets of clubs saying, "Yeah, he fucked off and left me. He didn't love me. He just couldn't deal with love. He was too fucked up to know how to love me." Now, how did that happen? What was it about this unlovable century that convinced us we were, despite everything, eminently lovable as a people, as a species? What made us think that anyone who fails to love us is damaged, lacking, malfunctioning in some way?

But I disagree. I think that surely, for every girl feeling entitled to love, there are a hundred thousand girls who do not feel entitled to anything. I think there are a hundred thousand girls crying in club bathrooms because they have been in love and love has not treated them kindly. I think none of us feel that we deserve love, and that few of us have been given a kind love, and that our hearts are broken or cracked in consequence. I think that those cracks are worthy of being seen and honored.

I will never have anything new to say about heartbreak. Nothing that has not already been said a thousand times by thousands of brilliant women. I can only say that I wish us the healing of the zebrafish, and I believe in it. I believe it with the full power of my broken heart.

India's Sons

Recently I stumbled across an art piece by one of my favorite artists, Jenny Holzer. It says, simply: "I am awake in the place where women die." Holzer created it after hearing about Bosnian war crimes, but I was struck by its universal applicability. As a woman living in Delhi today, it echoes in my ears. This is one of the places where women die.

After the brutal gang rape, disembowelment, and murder of a twenty-three-year-old physiotherapy intern on a bus in Delhi in 2012, journalists everywhere were asking one question: why does rape (more specifically, gang rape) occur so frequently in India? The corrupt police force; the inefficient judiciary; the social context of the systematic devaluation of women; the violence of enforced hyper masculinity; caste politics; poverty are all crucial pieces of the puzzle to understand why rape occurs. There are sociological answers, but these are not satisfactory. We might as well question the very existence of evil.

Short of murder, it's hard to imagine a crime more abhorrent than rape. When you rape somebody, you enter their body in one form or another without permission. There is nothing more taboo, more horrific, than that kind of violation. Which is perhaps why shows like *Game of Thrones* (and several classic Bollywood movies) use rape so frequently as a plot device. Picture men in writers' rooms all over the world brainstorming ideas for character development. "Something horrible has to happen to her . . . Oh, I know! She gets raped." We can't imagine anything worse happening to a person while they're still alive.

In the aftermath of the Delhi gang rape, it was extremely difficult for the men who had committed the rape to find lawyers willing to represent them, as public sentiment inclined to the view that these men were monsters, inhuman. We refuse to recognize that we have anything in common with them. In a controversial documentary called *India's Daughter*, filmmaker Leslee Udwin interviewed one of the men on the bus, Mukesh Singh. He describes the rape in graphic terms, but there is no emotion on his face—even when he speaks of his friends reaching into Nirbhaya's body, essentially disembowelling her with their bare hands.

When he is asked about his role in the murder, he repeats, "I drove the bus," admitting his involvement but also declining responsibility. Each of the six men blamed each other in their police statements. *It wasn't me who did that; it was him. I raped her, but I didn't kill her. I merely drove the bus.*

This is called "the bystander effect." Experiments show that when the number of individuals present in a room increases, their willingness to help decreases. If X is drowning and you are the only person present, you're much more likely to jump in the water than when Y and Z are also standing there, because now you have the luxury of thinking "saving X isn't my job." Violence works similarly. Even as you commit it, you are able to distance yourself from it. You think to yourself, "Well, even if I stopped, the other people will continue." (Which isn't, in fact, true.) But it's a logical fallacy that allows us the luxury of thinking our individual actions don't matter.

There is another theory that may help to explain what happened on the bus that night. In his book *Violence and the Sacred*, French scholar René Girard suggests that desire is not individually generated. We teach each other what to desire. When multiple individuals desire an object, a struggle breaks out and it can only end if the object is extinguished. If two or more men desire a woman, they choose to act in concert—to eliminate her to reduce their own appetite for violence. When Nirbhaya was left naked on the road, the man who found her said she looked like a cow that had just given birth. Thus, a woman becomes an animal to be sacrificed.

This theory is merely a technical way of saying that the men raping Nirbhaya weren't sadists. When we think of killers, we imagine them in the language of pop culture: they are men armed with scalpels. They torture their victims slowly and with deliberation. But that doesn't sound like the story the men on the bus told. What happened on the bus wasn't about sex or even about calculated cruelty. The men say, "I don't know what I was doing." I believe it. They didn't have a plan of any kind. This was violence at its most casual: they put their hands on (and in) her body because it was there. It became, briefly, a repository for the base desires they held as a group. Maybe it even seemed like a bonding ritual. Like something men do together. Before they got on that bus, they were separate individuals with separate destinies but that was about to change irrevocably. I wonder when they realized it. Was it when they raped her? When they beat her male companion? When they washed the blood off the seats of the bus, when they decided to throw her clothes out, they must have realized they were united forever in the knowledge of their collective guilt.

As I watched *India's Daughter*, it struck me that none of Nirbhaya's killers had lived a particularly privileged life. They came from poor backgrounds and were struggling to make a living. That night, they were drunk. Perhaps they felt the natural aggression of the poor in a country that constantly reminds them of what they cannot have. Women are marketed as just another commodity to them, after all. One buys and sells and barters away one's daughters.

Perhaps, they felt they had nothing to lose.

* * *

Two years later, another brutal gang rape shook the country. In May 2014, two Dalit girls were found hanging from a mango tree in Katra, Uttar Pradesh. They had been abducted from the village fields where they had gone to relieve themselves, as they had no toilet in their home. They had been gang-raped before they were strangled, and their bodies were left swaying in the breeze, mute villagers the only witness.

The girls murdered in Katra had been raped by upper-caste men—Yadavs. In the book *Life as a Dalit: Views from the Bottom on Caste in India*, Subhadra Mitra Channa points out that, "Women's bodies have forever been the sites of contestation of power from men of different groups." According to Manu, the lawgiver, all men have been granted the right of sexual access to women from castes lower than their own. "Untouchable" women are women who may be raped but who cannot otherwise be touched for fear of pollution. Again, this is a mentality that has little to do with desire and more with entitlement. It's not about what men desire but what they can get away with. Who you see as human; who you don't.

Then Uttar Pradesh chief minister, Akhilesh Yadav, described the Katra murders as though it were an unfortunate incident.[1] A month earlier, Mulayam Singh Yadav, then head of the Samajwadi Party, had told the press that he was opposed to the execution of rapists, saying "boys will be boys."[2] M.L. Sharma, defence lawyer in the Nirbhaya case, had blamed the incident on the victim, saying:

"If you keep sweets on the street, dogs will come to eat them. Why was Nirbhaya out so late at night?" He added: "Indian culture is the best culture [. . .]. In our culture, there is no place for a woman."[3] *Tehelka* published an undercover investigation of police attitudes toward rape. One officer said: "There are [rape] cases, but 70 percent involve consensual sex." He added, "Only if someone sees, or the money is denied, it gets turned into rape."[4]

It is hard to read these quotes with anything other than despair. I am confronted with the truth that we do not merely allow sexual violence against women, but also we sanction it, ensuring that it is repeated again and again until it becomes ritual.

* * *

Whenever one of these horrific crimes against women occurs, outrage takes familiar forms. We call Nirbhaya "India's daughter," by which we mean that we can all relate to her—that she represents *us* in some way. It's a cheap sop to our conscience. Women's bodies are their own. They exist in themselves; they represent nothing except what they are. Why do we feel so comfortable claiming them? It feels eerily familiar to conflate individual women with India as a whole. It reminds me of primary school classes, in which my teachers taught me that India ought to be referred to as Mother India. "See," my teacher said, "how the shape of the country looks like a woman in a sari, with Jammu and Kashmir as her crown." I looked, but I couldn't see it.

Women as martyrs; women's bodies representing the country; woman being the universal nurturer—I'm tired of it all. Nirbhaya doesn't have to belong to us to be respected. Women don't have to be good to be spared. They don't have to be our mothers or our sisters or our daughters for us to relate to them. Men are allowed complexity; we excuse their bad behavior and sweep the history of their sins under the rug (no matter how much it costs us to do so).

Instead of bending over to accommodate men's bad behavior, can we not prioritize women? Can we not afford women complexity for once?

If we can't, the least we can do is allow them to exist in peace. Once, I wrote about how men should leave women alone on the street and was immediately beset by angry, defensive men. "You feminists!" they cried. "You can't even approach women in public spaces. Women automatically assume you have bad intentions. They're offended by everything we do. What are we supposed to, never talk to women?" My only answer to that is: "Yes. If you can't figure out how to approach women respectfully, leave them alone. Never talk to them if you can't do so without offending them."

Leaving people alone is perhaps the noblest thing you can do for them. Being left alone is a luxury women are rarely afforded.

Even in death, their bodies were exposed to the public gaze, as I am reminded every time I look at news articles of the murdered girls in Katra. The photographs show the girls' faces; the photographer does not even have the grace to censor their faces. Their death is a spectacle and so we stare, transfixed, at what we have wrought. At the fruits of what we have planted.

* * *

It is easy, in the face of unspeakable violence, to analyze it as an anomaly. To declare that the men on the bus were monsters. If it was an anomaly, that means that we—safe, comfortable in our homes—are not complicit. But as I write this, six years after Nirbhaya's murder, it feels like an evasion.

These were not monsters or boys being boys. These were men raised in a world where violence against women is nothing out of the ordinary. Nirbhaya was given the title "India's daughter." But it is not enough to claim the victim without claiming the perpetrator. Look, India. Turn your gazes away from the women you call your daughters. Remember, these are your sons.

Wolves

I have always loved fairy tales. Not the sweetened versions told by the Brothers Grimm, but the dark, raw stories that predate them. These stories are honest about the sacrifices that people make for happy endings. (The ugly stepsisters cut off their toes to fit into the crystal slippers, and when they are found out, they are executed by Cinderella's sweet prince.)

"Red Riding Hood" is one of the few stories that, even in Grimm form, is dark. Like all fairy tales, nobody knows the exact wording, but we recognize the main beats. Little girl. Red hood. A forest, a warning mother. A basket full of goodies. She strays off the path and in the darkness encounters a Big Bad Wolf. It is unclear what happens next, but in almost every story, it ends poorly for Red Riding Hood and her grandmother. *The better to eat you with, my dear.*

Was it Red's fault? Well, yes, likely. What was she doing in a place where she might encounter a wolf? The moral of the story— Charles Perrault points this out in his book, so we are left with no doubt—is that wolves are everywhere, looking to prey on young girls. In this story, the "wolf" is a metaphor for a *rapist*.

I can't remember the first time I was warned not to go outside after dark. But I know it must have happened because this is a scene from my childhood.

Long grasses in the park. A jut of cliff overhead. Sun beginning to recede as the boys bash in the field to find a lost cricket ball.

A shout goes up. They want to play another game.

I look up at the setting sun.

No, I say. *I have to go home. I'm not allowed out after dark.*

They shrug. It is nothing to them what I am allowed and not allowed to do. They continue the game as I turn and trudge back home—it is only a two-minute walk from the park, after all.

The world is full of wolves, there is no denying.

Every girl has certain stories of wolves that she can recount. Some of these start as early as she can remember. I am a little luckier—the first incident I remember is a man watching me walk home from school with his binoculars from the upper story of his house. I think, though I am not sure, he was an old man, who kept his perversions to this: watching young girls in their school uniforms.

I am lucky. That particular wolf was toothless. Others were not as edentulate, from the man who tried to pull my blankets down as I (a twelve-year-old) slept in the Rajdhani Express to the man who pulled his cock out and masturbated in front of me as I left my law office. The wolves that we read about every day—the ones that gang-rape girls and leave them for dead, or set them on fire, or throw them into village wells, or leave them swaying from mango trees—have claws and teeth and do not hesitate to use them. I don't need to talk about those wolves because you know all about them already.

How do you guard against a wolf? Build a house with strong bricks. Lock the doors and windows.

I first came to Delhi when I was eighteen years old. I was enrolled abroad but my parents wanted me to see what St. Stephen's was like.

It's the best college in the country, they told me. I was quite prepared to believe it. It was beautiful—in the dingy way that so many buildings in India are. The wide sweep of the quad, the red and yellow brick walls, the particular taste of the mince cutlets and the powdery green chutney in the cafeteria—and I was willing to be enchanted by it. They were enough to occupy my center and my periphery. I knew very little of Delhi outside of my college and I didn't care to know more.

"Are you staying with your parents or do you stay in the rez?" a girl asked me, before explaining that "rez" was shorthand for the residence halls. If I were staying in the rez, I had to be back by no later than 10 P.M.

I was confused by this information. College boys didn't have the freedom to go out after ten? That was an absurd curfew. I thought of the boys I was used to in America, how they threw all-night parties in their Amherst dorms and their UMass frats.

"Oh, no. They can stay out all night. Girls have to be back by ten. Because, you know, this is a dangerous city for women."

I nodded. Of course. It made sense to have different rules for us because we experienced the world differently. It didn't matter that at eighteen we were barely women—all of us were girls—but we could be grouped with women and in that lay the danger.

Sri Sairam Engineering College: Special Instructions for Girls, September 2015

Big 'Nos' for Girls

1. No Leggings/tight pants and tops
2. No Short Kurtha
3. No Knot type (Backside) tops
4. No 'Lose Hair' hairdo
5. No big stud or earring
6. NO very high heels or fancy slippers
7. NO Patiala/Anarkali (Which will hide leggings) & high fancy dresses with netted design
8. No hair colouring
9. NO transparent & short dupatta
10. No birthday/new year celebrations inside college campus
11. Should not bring sweets/chocolates or any other snacks in bulk quantities inside college campus to share with friends
12. No loitering on corridor unnecessarily
13. Should not enter into other classes during class hours for borrowing Books, Lab Coats, and other items
14. No pendrive/mobile
15. No two/four wheeler
16. NO account in Facebook, Whatsapp, and other related types of this kind
17. Should follow allotted staircases and corridors
18. Should not talk to boy students [sic]

There are always "special instructions for girls." For boys, it is enough to address them *with* girls. What applies to boys is universal, such as cheating or bullying or speaking out of turn in class, which are also forbidden to girls. But over and above the general rules, we must have some extra ones for girls. The more, the better—we wouldn't want to miss anything, to leave a single loophole that would render our girls unsafe.

"We are going to have a special class today," announces my teacher bossily in the eighth grade. "This class is only for girls. Boys will go to a separate room with the PT teacher." Her spectacles quiver as she says it and we look at each other in wonder. The announcement has the vague air of a treat, and treats are not commonplace at my school.

What it meant, as we discovered, was forty-five minutes in the AV room, where she played a video on menstruation. It was scrubbed of any mentions of sex and merely cautioned that we might get our periods at any time. If we did, we were to wear a thing called a sanitary napkin. Also, we were to be very careful about consorting with boys from now on. *How* exactly consorting with boys was related to menstruation, we were not informed of.

After the class, I approached a boy student (almost immediately breaking the video's diktats) and begged him to tell me what they had done in the last hour. What was the equivalent of menstruation for girls: something so secret they must have a separate room to discuss it in?

He shrugged. "We played dodgeball with the PT coach."

What is the moral of this story?

Living in Delhi today, says a friend, is like living in a petri dish. We are constantly hovering on the edge of change. Raggedy areas of the city become gentrified, then fall out of favor again. We use apps for almost everything, and all the global-chain restaurants are marching irrevocably into the city. Young people have new professions these days: "lifestyle blogger" and "event curator." Driving into Gurgaon on a Friday afternoon, you can watch the landscape as it mutates, an iridescent bubble of skyscrapers and heat. Progress, measured by the tick of each crane in the sky.

And yet, I press my face against the glass of the cab I'm in as it drives home, noting the complete absence of women on the roads.

After 11 P.M., most areas in Delhi–NCR morph into men-only zones. Men slouch against the trees, smoking Gold Flake cigarettes, spreading blankets against the December chill, rubbing chili powder over fresh corn on the flame, or buying their rajma-chawal dinners. Men take shortcuts through the parks at night. Men sleep on the footpaths and wander through the lonely underpasses in Defence Colony. Men run for the late-night bus and sit next to the other men on board. Men squat on the street, piss, and then stand up again in the sure knowledge that it doesn't matter if their genitalia is on display. In fact, they prefer it—adjusting their penises lightly through the cloth of their lungis. The only visible women on the street are the ones on hoardings, smiling eerily (Priyanka Chopra selling diamonds and shampoo).

One night, I remember that I have to buy a bottle of wine. I decide to stop at Khan Market, at the only government wine and beer shop in that area.

Everyone turns as I walk in—their faces are amazed and disapproving. I am the only woman in the shop, and this confers a queer kind of notoriety on me. In the jostle and hubbub, they make way for me to go to the counter. The shopkeeper asks me what I want before everybody else, recognizing that it isn't good to have a woman waiting too long in a men-only area. Women shouldn't be outside at night.

In her journals, Sylvia Plath writes:

Yes, my consuming desire is to mingle with road crews, sailors and soldiers, barroom regulars—to be a part of a scene, anonymous, listening, recording—all this is spoiled by the fact that I am a girl, a female always supposedly in danger of assault and battery. My consuming interest in men and their lives is often misconstrued as a desire to seduce them, or as an invitation to intimacy. Yes, God, I want to

talk to everybody as deeply as I can. I want to be able to sleep
in an open field, to travel west, to walk freely at night [. . .]

I think of it as I hurry across the sunlit paths. I can see it going
down now, the red sinking sun. I imagine what it would be like
to walk through the Lodhi tombs at night, to fall asleep propped
against a Gulmohar tree. To be, to walk, to exist unmolested in
the public sphere—is this not the most fundamental privilege that
should be accorded to human beings? Without it, what did I have
to brag of?

Sometimes, I long for a brief respite from this unceasing,
tiresome condition of being a woman. I long for it in the same
way as an invalid might wish a respite from illness.

It's not only me who has to suffer from this condition. Anybody
who is responsible for a woman—her father, her brothers, her
boyfriend, or perhaps her sons—has to bear the burden of her
unchanging vulnerability. Protect her from the wolves.

Sometimes, I look at my father and feel an odd twinge of
compassion. I think of the many, many, many fights that we have
fought over the years. About what I'm wearing, where I'm going,
who with and when I'll be back.

My father is not a naturally tyrannical person, unlike so many
brown fathers. He hates asking what I'm doing, who I'm going to
see. I can just tell.

Papa, *his voice rising a half-octave, in an effort to seem
nonchalant*: And . . . is that what you're wearing?

Me: Yes.

Papa, *struggles for a moment*: Take a shawl.

Take a shawl! How many desi women hear that every day? As
if it were a protective incantation.

Take a shawl. Take two shawls. You can change when you get
there. Carry a wrap. Don't you want to carry a wrap? It's chilly out
(*it is not chilly out*). Adjust your dupatta so it covers your bosom.

Just pull your skirt down until you reach the party. A jacket will go with that very well, don't you think? Until you reach, only until you reach. Then you can change.

I remember asking one of my girlfriends in St. Stephen's how her strict mother allowed her to wear miniskirts every day. She replied that she changed in the car: her trousers were left in the backseat.

I think of women all over India—young girls, mostly, but surely there are older women too—who are adept at buttoning up their blazers while they wave goodbye to their parents or who stuff a dupatta under the loose brick in their garden so they can put it back on when they come in at night. Underneath, these women are wearing tank tops, halters that flash silver in the club, or brief shirts that expose a sliver of stomach over jeans. I think of what a perfect metaphor it is for the double life that Indian women are forced to live.

And yet, I do understand my father's worry, the worry of all Indian parents everywhere. I try to think of what it would be like to have a daughter: to raise something so precious in a world of wolves. Even in my more exasperated moments, I am well able to imagine the desire to lock up one's daughter in the high tower. To set dragons outside so that she is safe.

How do we keep our girls safe?

There are any number of politicians who claim to have the answer. Samajwadi Party leader Abu Azmi went on record to say that scantily clad women attract male attention and that rape cases are on the rise due to "women wearing less clothes." A female politician, Asha Mirje, had the same explanation: "Rapes take place also because of a woman's clothes, her behavior, and her being at inappropriate places." Mirje's comment is my favorite: raising as it does the question of what an "appropriate place" is. Since there is no consensus, perhaps we ought to pass an ordinance making it perfectly clear:

Appropriate Place for a Woman
1) Home

Inappropriate Place:
1) Outside Home

Perhaps, the winner is the khap panchayat of Haryana's Jind district, that blames chowmein for rape: "[. . .] consumption of fast food contributes to such incidents. Chowmein leads to hormonal imbalance evoking an urge to indulge in such acts," and, "You also know the impact of chowmein, which is a spicy food, on our body. Hence, our elders also advised to consume light and nutritious food." I read these extraordinary statements as I eat the momos that I've bought for 30 rupees from the food stall in the corner. I dip the momos in the fiery red sauce that feels like it's burning my small intestines. I wait for any hormonal changes to make themselves apparent.

The khap aside, the most common dictum—all over the world—seems to be that women should avoid going to dangerous places. In Delhi, they tell me to stay away from West Delhi, Hauz Khas Village, Munirka, and Paharganj, among others. These are lawless places, where our safety is not guaranteed. They recount stories to me with wide eyes as if my body were no more substantial than a wisp of cotton. As if I could be snatched away by anybody who wanted to snatch me.

Even in Boston, a taxi driver whistles in alarm as we tell him where we want to go.

"Roxbury? No, ma'am. I'm not taking two young girls to Roxbury at this hour. Don't want to see your faces in the paper tomorrow. Know what I mean? What do you girls want to go to Roxbury for, anyway?"

Yes, there are any number of men telling us what we should do to escape the wolves outside the gate. They are like Red Riding Hood's mother, marking out a safe path for us. Often, that path is no path at all. If Red Riding Hood had never gone out, nothing bad could have happened.

What does a wolf look like?

My favorite urban legend is the story of the babysitter. Have you heard that one? A young woman on a babysitting job begins to receive strange phone calls. A man is watching her. Worried, she telephones the police, who say they will trace the calls. When they do, they tell her to get out—the calls are coming from inside the house.

The shocking twist is what Indian men don't want to admit: the wolves are already inside the gates. We think of our homes as safe, insulated. Clean as a lick of white paint in the afternoon sun. But what happens inside is deadly, and what can happen inside is *everything*. Inside the four walls of the house, fathers touch daughters, brothers rape sisters, and uncles prey on little girls. Husbands rape their wives with impunity, knowing that they are protected by the law. In-laws burn the new bride for not paying enough dowry. Women who are pregnant with their girl children are dragged to clinics to get abortions. Teenagers who fall in love with boys from different castes are killed for the sake of the families' mythical honor. These wolves are not the ones we have been taught to recognize; these are not wolves mentioned in storybooks. When these wolves come, there is nobody who will believe that they are wolves.

I turn on Mira Nair's *Monsoon Wedding* and watch as the young girl Aliya speaks forlornly of her uncle touching her while the rest of her family are astonished. She does not even accuse him. She has not learned that it is wrong for men to make her feel bad in that way. Most women never learn that. And does it matter, when we are not believed?

I tell a friend about a certain man we both know. I say not that he is a bad man, but that he has done a "bad thing." I describe the "bad thing" delicately, making sure not to exaggerate. (Women are natural lawyers—even in our accusations we make sure not to go too far. We punctuate each soft statement with a disclaimer, as if we couldn't trust our eyes or senses.)

My friend is astonished. I can see it in his eyes—a flickering disbelief. A wonderment. He is struggling to believe me; I know he wants to believe me. With a little effort (like the queen from *Alice in Wonderland* who can believe impossible things), he manages it.

Later he says, *living in the world of women is like . . . I don't know. Like being on another planet. The craziest things happen to you.*

I am a little hurt by his statement, but I know what he means. Living as a woman does feel like alchemy. You can—with a touch of your finger—transform a good man into a monster. You can see a wolf in a regular man when you're alone together and he reaches for you. You will be privy to things other men can never know.

Is that a reward?

If a man is a wolf, what are we—us girls, waiting in our houses, soft, so soft and tender and unused to cruelty? Are we destined to be lambs?

I grow obsessed with revenge fantasies. I do not watch ordinary, sweet-edged movies, the kind they show in every multiplex. I seek out and obsessively consume the darkest movies I can find, in which terrible things happen to women. In which women do terrible things as revenge. I eat popcorn, shoving the kernels frantically into my mouth as Jennifer disembowels a man on *I Spit on Your Grave*. I wonder briefly if I have some kind of disorder but push the worry aside. I consider the words of James Baldwin and think that to live as an Indian woman is to live in a constant state of rage.

One night, two men come up to my friend and me on the street. It is late and we are at my car, just unlocking the door.

He is drunk, one of the men. He says to my friend—who is small and pretty and who looks incredibly nervous—*I want to talk to you for a moment.*

No, she says politely, and gets in the car.

He says something else. It is not mean or hostile but I do not care. For that moment, I am not myself. I walk forward and look at him squarely in the face. We are the same height, although his shoulders are much broader than mine. I think of what I've learned in MMA—oh yes, I've taken self-defence, I've done the things they told me to do as protection—about combat. Two opponents must be roughly the same size to be evenly matched. Other things (fitness level; knowledge of technique) *do* count, but a small fighter will generally always lose against a larger opponent.

I push him. It is a hard push, the kind of push that says I am not afraid. I know at that moment that I am not. I am reckless, filled with a delicious recklessness that does not care whether I live or die. I see fear in the man's eyes and am delighted that I have the ability to cause fear.

"Please," says his friend uselessly. "Please."

They talk to me soothingly, their hands fluttering like doves above their shirt collars in the universal symbol for truce. I allow them to coax me into dropping it. I have been—many times—on the other side of this equation. Trying to talk men out of violence. Tugging on their shirts, sweetening my tone so that they simmer down.

"Never," I say, "scare women like that again."

He promises. There is something—if not humility, then its cousin—in his eyes. I stride back to my car, full of power. If, I think, I have to live in this dangerous world, I commit to living in it fully. I will not always look over my shoulder. I will sometimes push men back the way they push me. I accept the bittersweet risk of it all. While I live, I will not live a life that is lesser than men's, not more circumscribed. I will not accept more rules than they do.

Finally, I read other versions of "Red Riding Hood." My favorites are the ones in which she escapes without anybody's help—not the woodcutter's, not anybody's. In those versions, the wolf sometimes survives, but it is the girl I am thinking of. Later, I think, she might have come back with an axe, to the rosy wood, and murdered the wolf. Or perhaps not. I like to think that she might have come back. I sit on my roof and watch the thousand keen-eyed stars in the hot night and dream that there is another world in which there are no wolves. There are only a thousand Red Riding Hoods, each skipping through the rosy woods, sure and certain that they will reach their destinations, innocent in the heartless way of children who never have to grow up too soon.

Jane Doe

"Darkling I listen; and, for many a time/I have been half in
love with easeful Death [. . .]"

—"Ode to a Nightingale," John Keats

I have seen a picture of Afton Elaine Burton with Charles Manson
that haunts my imagination.

I am not surprised to discover she is beautiful. Her dark, center-
parted hair is drawn around the serene face of a Jane Birkin-type,
Raphaelite Madonna. She stands slightly behind her fiancé, her
hands gripping his arms like a talisman, as though he is her lucky
star. "But Star is *her* nickname [emphasis added]," he says. In an
interview with *Rolling Stone*, he says she is not a woman but a star
in the Milky Way. Burton is very young—only twenty-six—and I
wonder how long she's been in love with the devil.

* * *

I'm thirteen years old, staying up late to watch *Scream* on television
even though I've seen it twice already. My mother comes in during
my favorite scene, the opening, in which Drew Barrymore plays

the blonde sweater-princess who gets a phone call from Ghostface. Ghostface announces his intention to gut her like a fish, and my mother is dismayed.

"Why do you watch this stuff?" she says, shaking her head. My mother likes romantic comedies. "It's not normal. You'll get nightmares."

"I already *have* nightmares, Ma," I say blankly. It's true. My nightmares predate horror movies. Every night, like Clarice Starling, I'd wake up hearing the screaming of the lambs. Do you still remember the nightmares you had as a child that make you afraid even as an adult?

I know she worries that there is a darkness in my head. Isn't this every parent's fear: that their children will grow into people they cannot understand?

That is what I grow into: a person obsessed with hurt. I read about serial killers. I look up transcripts of old interviews with people on death row in Texas. I save images of what they request as their final meals. I watch every episode of *Dexter*. When I have to write a paper for my homicide investigations class in law school, I choose to write about the Long Island serial killer, an unidentified man who killed ten sex workers over a period of twenty years.

None of it desensitizes me to violence. I am still as gripped and tortured by violence as though I am viewing it afresh each time. When I read the details of the crimes that men commit against women, I feel the urge to share the suffering, and in doing so lessen it. Quickly, the abstract knife becomes the knife sliding into *my* belly; *my* skull cracking like a faint egg on an indifferent countertop. The wounding of the flesh consumes a space in my mind I dare not enter.

The first time I ordered steak in an expensive restaurant, I ordered it well-done, to the waiter's evident disapproval. I need my meat to look like things other than meat. I am afraid of coming too close to the bone. I looked at my neighbor's plate: the unexpected, shocking pink of a rare steak, slipping a little down a pristine plate. I carved a slice of the tender meat off my own steak, looking for all the world like an everyday steak-eater.

This, I thought, was akin to how serial killers cut into flesh—with dexterity and enjoyment. Perhaps there is effort involved in the wounding, but it is the indifference to pain that sets them apart from regular human beings. I dwell on it with masochistic regularity every time I read a gruesome headline or catch a story on the nightly news, and always, *always*, think about the killer. I conjugate irregular verbs in the class of evil.

How could he do that
How could they do that
How could he have done that
How could she have done that (more rarely)
How could they have done that

This need to eviscerate evil is something I accept with equanimity, the way somebody else might accept a need to avoid cracks in the sidewalk. We all live with the frail parts of our personality, and this is mine: a crippling longing to track evil to its home, to strip it to its fundament. To dissolve it, and in doing so, escape it.

* * *

The ways in which we write about serial killers is predictable as pain itself.

Take Hannibal Lecter, Thomas Harris's brainchild, the public darling, the genius in popular imagination. Hannibal is brilliant, a cultured genius with a taste for Chianti, attractive female detectives, and other people's brains chopped up with fava beans. He possesses every attribute that we root for: an origin story. An explanation for his depravity. A magnetic, brooding presence. A redemptive arc.

These are the ways in which we write about serial killers. What caused this charming young man to hurt these girls? What could it possibly be, the source of this darkness that spirals out beyond him? What is it? The spotlight remains firmly on Jack the Ripper while the girls he murdered are relegated to the London fog. In *True Detective*, the victims are spread-eagled, splayed, flayed. Left naked in grotesque poses, they are a mere blip on the horizon of the story. They exist because victims must exist, but the locus of the story is not in their wounded bodies. The site of the story is in their fascinating killer: the Yellow King.

The victims of a serial killer are always elusive as smoke from a gun fired by somebody else; they exist in the shadowy places as statistics. Their humanity is taken from them when their life is taken and their personality erased in the service of justice. Scrapbook: victim #1, victim #8, victim #13. Jane Doe. If they are identified, their families remember them and their hometowns confer grisly fame on them forever. But even when they are identified, they remain Jane Doe, grouped together in the Wikipedia entry for Ted Bundy, floating facelessly in a dark pool where "victim" comes before their names forever.

What is clear—with painful clarity—is that we, the public, are no less fascinated by the image of Charles Manson than Afton Elaine Barton. We all find evil fascinating but shudder at the knowledge that some people will marry it because they are drawn to its dark, bloated edges in the same way that we are. This is the notoriety that anybody can possess in the twenty-first century, if they have a knife and are willing to gut women like fish. They may be punished, they may not, but afterwards, there will always be people who seek them out, write obsessively about them, examine their motives with as much fervor as if they were Napoleon. When the truth is, there is nothing extraordinary about the mind of a serial killer. Not any more than there is anything extraordinary about a cracked window. There is a ripple, a break in the glass psyche, a defect. A presence of the desire to cause pain; an absence of empathy. No more, no less.

* * *

There is no resolution to my story of wound excavation, no illumination that shows the way anyone has to go to bury their demons. A woman has to have a code, though. Maybe this is mine; maybe it's not about figuring out evil. Maybe it's enough to talk about the hurt woman; maybe it's enough to remember her specific story and to tell it again and again so that it is not forgotten. She, too, is mortal and precious. More extraordinary than the darkness that surrounds her. If only she could remain.

What Is Dark in Me Illumine

I had a puppy once, Max, whom I loved dearly. Max was not like other dogs; he was the quietest puppy in the cage when I saw him.

There were three spaniels in the cage. One, an enthusiastic girl, another, an aggressive boy, and the third cowered in the back, completely silent. I picked him up, and the man selling the dogs assured me that I wouldn't regret it.

He was quite right, though he'd only been gassing in the hope of making a sale. Max turned out to be one of the sweetest dogs in the entire kingdom of Sweet Dogs. He never barked, he never bit. He could never find anything (despite the hunting reputation of his species). He mostly just napped. Even if you shouted "Kitty! Look, Max! There's a kitty!" in his ear, he would look mournfully at you as if refusing to take the bait.

I tried to teach him how to use the toilet early on. All he had to do was nudge and paw at the door until someone let him into the garden. But, of course, it took some doing. For a while, I had to clean his piss whenever I found it (his favorite spot was under a chair in the living room). Annoyed, I turned to manuals on dog-training.

"Your dog knows when it has done something wrong," intoned the manual. "In order to teach it discipline, rub its nose in the puddle. This will be punishment enough to prevent future disobedience."

Rub its nose in the puddle? This seemed a little extreme for my taste, but I reckoned it was worth a go. After all, Max was a filth-merchant. A regular mess-maker. There was nothing he loved more than rolling around in mud and sludge. Perhaps, he wouldn't mind the scent of his own pee so much.

The next time I glimpsed a spreading yellow puddle under the settee, I called Max sternly. He came—at once—with the abject look of a puppy who knows he has done something wrong. Droopy ears drooping further, eyes even more mournful than usual. I hardened my heart and dragged him by the collar to the offending puddle.

"See that? SEE THAT? That's your fault. You're a bad boy, Max. A BAD BOY."

He quivered. But my mind was made up.

I shoved his head hard—he was only a small-to-medium dog—into the puddle. "A BAD BOY. SMELL THAT? THAT'S YOUR FAULT. YOU SHOULDN'T HAVE DONE THAT. YOU'RE A BAD DOG."

When I judged he'd finally had enough, I let go. He jumped back from the puddle immediately and looked at me.

That look! As long as I live and breathe, I will never forget that look. It transfixed me with its honesty. His brown eyes had a look of infinite sorrow. Those eyes blamed me not in the least—dogs rarely reproach humans—but they seemed to ask me why. Wincing, drooping, full of new pain—I'd *hurt* him.

With a little cry, I gathered him into my arms and took him out of the room. I hugged and kissed and petted him, trying to convey in doggy terms that I was sorry and that I'd never betray him again. He submitted patiently to my hugs.

I cleaned up the puddle on my own. (He rarely made a mess inside the house after that day.)

When Max died—thirteen years after I had picked him out of a pet-shop cage—I thought of that day. Dogs' memories are limited—a tiny sandbox in a vast space—and yet, I wondered if he remembered it too. If in his dim consciousness, he remembered what I'd done to him.

The events of that day came as a revelation to me, if not to Max. (Dogs are not altogether surprised by the waywardness of human beings.) It struck me for the first time that I was capable of real harshness, real cruelty. It does not seem momentous to me now that I am older, but I can remember how it stung: the knowledge that I was capable of being cruel. That I was capable of rubbing a whimpering, traumatized dog's nose in his own piss. This too was me.

Nearly twenty years after that day, I settled down on that same couch to read a book about domestic abuse. The book grappled with the question of why men beat their wives and how society could prevent it. I read it with some vague preconceptions of my own; I assumed the cause was some complicated cocktail of genetics and upbringing. The book said *yes*, it was one of the reasons. But it also—and this part surprised me, I remember—said that it was because the women were there.

> There is no guaranteed way for a victim to escape being abused by her husband. One of the best solutions is for the victim to simply not be there. Not be in the kitchen or in the drawing room when her husband comes home drunk and raging. If she can absent herself during that crucial window of time in which he is violent [. . .] she can avoid an otherwise certain fate.

The book explained that domestic abusers were usually men who felt disenfranchised in the world or emasculated. They often felt powerless at work or oppressed by people in more powerful positions than them. They may have endured shouting or public humiliation at work. And yet, they never retaliated against their bosses or against the oppressive forces they encountered in their daily lives. They took out their rage on what they felt were "legitimate targets."

The Monkey Experiment

A primatologist at Stanford locked five monkeys in a cage. As he expected, the monkeys soon established a hierarchy of dominance through fighting. Monkey #1 beat monkey #2, monkey #2 beat monkey #3, and so on. The winner was the monkey with the highest testosterone.

The primatologist took a mid-ranging monkey—monkey #3—out of the cage and injected him with a hefty dose of testosterone. Enough to challenge monkey #1 for dominance. But contrary to expectation, monkey #3 turned savagely on monkeys #4 and #5. The ones who had already been established as beneath him.

Violence Is Transferable

There is a strongly held cultural belief that men are kind to women. That is to say, there is a belief that men are kinder to women than they are to other men. Chivalry. Courtesy. Notions of being a "gentleman." These are all ideals that are fed to us with our milk as babies. We girls grow fat and intoxicated on these lies.

Oh, I'm not talking of commonplace politeness. Of that, men have plenty. They pull out chairs for me and hold doors. They usher me to this place and that. No doubt many of them would offer me a jacket if I said that I was cold. (How much of this is because I am still young and conventionally attractive, I do not care to speculate. I do not speculate whether they would offer these common courtesies to women they find unattractive.) But the truth is that none of this is kindness. Whatever you think is kindness to other people—treating them with dignity, not raising your voices at them, not insulting or mocking or hurting them—is not how men treat women.

I learned this early, on the day the dhobi's wife came to work with the marks of the hot iron on her forehead. It was a drinking day for him, she explained dispassionately. This was nothing unusual to her and indeed only the first of many leaves she'd take. (*Unwell* always meant that she'd suffered a particularly bad beating the night before.) There was ordinary or garden-variety cruelty, and then there was attempting to iron someone's face. But before long, I would be familiar with every form of cruelty that men inflicted on women.

Men slapping women. Punching them. Kicking them down the stairs. Pinching, pulling, pushing, poking, prodding, and prying. Screaming so loudly at them that the whole neighborhood could hear. Screaming insults at them. Hurling obscenities at strange women on the street. Men calling women ugly, slattern, worthless. Men calling women mad. Following women to murmur obscenities at them. Throwing acid on their faces when they rebuffed your advances. Men raping women. Men gang-raping women. Sexually harassing women. Men leering at women, subjecting them to a stare so hard it felt like hatred. Groping them on crowded subways and buses. Men keeping women at home by force. Men tying women to the bed, or keeping them captive in tiny rooms for days. Kicking women in the stomach. Men videotaping women in dressing rooms, setting cameras to spy on them, or watching with binoculars as girls no older than twelve walked home from school. Publicly humiliating women. Slut-shaming women. Sharing child porn. Forcing little girls into marriages. Men burning women for dowry. Men stabbing, strangling, choking women who brought "dishonor to the family." Men interrogating women on where they were going. Men not allowing women to go anywhere. Men punishing women who spoke about their mistreatment. Men slut shaming the survivors of rape, and also those who did not survive it. Men hurting women in a hundred thousand ways, in a million uncountable ways, and every day finding new places to hurt women.

Other writers—better writers, sharp social commentators and feminist theorists—explain, in excruciating detail, what it *is* that makes these men hurt women. It's their backgrounds; it's in the culture they are imbibing (a culture that objectifies women constantly); it's in the lessons they learn from their elders.

Reading all this feels a little like watching a TV show about a serial killer. (You, the gaping audience, are watching two maverick detectives say things like, "Well, the perpetrator was clearly unsuccessful with women . . .")

I am not satisfied with the answers they provide, even though I understand that these are objectively good answers. To me, it so often seems like men hurt women because they *can*. Because the women are there, and because it's easier to hurt women than other men. Women are generally softer, smaller, less physically strong. Not in all cases, of course, but even when women are strong, they are less likely to hit back. Women do not often respond to verbal threats with physical aggression. Women do not threaten men with violence; they are much more likely to be on the receiving end of such threats.

It is easy to berate women in the workplace, I learn. One day at my law firm (I am one of only two women there and the only one present that day), I bring up the subject of corporations paying academic institutions to author research studies. I had not heard of this before. It is astounding to me and at once troubling that a tobacco company can pay a private institute to write a white paper on why smoking cigarettes isn't a bad thing. It seems immoral to me—an unsuspecting public has no idea of the nexus between the institute and the company.

I am, as I learn, the only person in the office to hold that opinion. Immediately four men descend on me, shouting their opinions on why I'm wrong, why it is "standard practice" to do this in the industry. It is not so much what they're saying, but the volume at which they're saying it. They are shouting so loudly that another colleague comes out of his office.

I am seated, they are towering over me. It is a neat reflection of where the authority lies.

It's so *easy.*

It's easy to berate women at home too. We see it all the time. We see it normalized on TV and in movies. Shouting that is not mere shouting but that is verbal abuse.

Here's a scene from the script of *Pulp Fiction* (1994). If you haven't seen it, Butch Coolidge (played by a hulking Bruce Willis) is looking for his father's gold watch. He asks his girlfriend, Fabienne (played by the physically slight Maria de Medeiros), where it is. When she cannot answer him, he begins to get angry.

Butch: Where's my watch?
Fabienne: It's there.
Butch: No, it's not. It's not here.
Fabienne: Have you looked?
By now, Butch is frantically rummaging through the suitcase.
Butch: Yes, I've fuckin' looked!
He's now throwing clothes.
Butch: What the fuck do you think I'm doing?! Are you sure you got it?
Fabienne can hardly speak, she's never seen Butch this way.
Fabienne: Uh . . . yes . . . beside the table drawer—
Butch:—on the little kangaroo.

Fabienne: Yes, it was on your little kangaroo.

Butch: Well it's not here!

Fabienne, *on the verge of tears*: Well it should be!

Butch: Oh, it most definitely should be here, but it's not. So where is it?

Fabienne is crying and scared.

Butch lowers his voice, which only makes him more menacing.

Butch: Fabienne, that was my father's fuckin' watch. You know what my father went through to get me that watch? . . . I don't wanna get into it right now . . . but he went through a lot. Now all this other shit, you coulda set on fire, but I specifically reminded you not to forget my father's watch. Now think, did you get it?

Fabienne: I believe so . . .

Butch: You believe so? You either did, or you didn't, now which one is it?

Fabienne: Then I did.

Butch: Are you sure?

Fabienne, *shaking*: No.

Butch freaks out, punches the air.

Fabienne screams and backs into a corner, Butch picks up the motel TV and throws it against the wall.

Fabienne screams in horror.

As a woman, this scene is intensely uncomfortable. It is all too real—Butch hits every single beat of the familiar male anger.

Male anger is like this: it doesn't erupt all at once. Not the abusive kind. It ramps up. At first, Butch asks questions. *Where is the watch?* He lowers his voice: *Do you know how much that watch meant to me?* Now pay attention as he switches to another question: *Did you get it?*

Fabienne answers as most of us would—I *thought* so. I *believe* so. Butch seizes on this opening to mock her. *Either you did or you didn't.* Berating a woman often involves calling her stupid. Insulting her intelligence. "Are you FUCKING stupid?" is what he's effectively saying here.

Finally, he freaks out. He punches the air. Then he picks up the TV and throws it across the room.

Men watch this scene mostly unperturbed. They may recognize—at the mildest level—that Butch is upset. With legitimate reason, according to them (the movie has already established how important this watch is to Butch). But that's all. If you asked men whether Butch was being abusive, they would laugh off the suggestion. After all, he didn't hit *her* with the TV, did he? He didn't even throw it in her direction. And yet, what's happened here? He's inflicting tremendous pain, fear, and trauma on his girlfriend. He's punching the air—a threat that he could punch her. He throws the TV across the room— another threat. I could throw this at you if I wanted to. Maybe *you're* next. Be afraid; be very, very afraid.

What happens next is equally enlightening: Butch is no longer angry.

Butch looks towards her, suddenly calm.
Butch, *to Fabienne*: No! It's not your fault. *approaches her*
You left it at the apartment.
He bends down in front of the woman who has sunk to the floor. He touches her hand, she flinches.
Butch: If you did leave it at the apartment, it's not your fault. I had you bring a bunch of stuff. I reminded you about it, but I didn't illustrate how personal the watch was to me. If all I gave a fuck about was my watch, I should've told you. You ain't a mind reader.
He kisses her hand. Then rises.
Fabienne is still sniffling.
Butch goes to the closet.

Fabienne: I'm sorry.

Butch puts on his high-school jacket.

Butch: Don't be. It just means I won't be able to eat breakfast with you.

Fabienne: Why does it mean that?

Butch: Because I'm going back to my apartment to get my watch.

Fabienne: Won't the gangsters be looking for you there?

Butch: That's what I'm gonna find out. If they are, and I don't think I can handle it, I'll split.

Rising from the floor.

Fabienne: I was so dreadful. I saw your watch, I thought I brought it. I'm so sorry.

Butch brings her close and puts his hands on her face.

Butch: Don't feel bad, sugar pop. Nothing you could ever do would make me permanently angry at you. *pause* I love you, remember? *he digs some money out of his wallet* Now here's some money, order those pancakes and have a great breakfast.

Fabienne: Don't go.

Butch: I'll be back before you can say blueberry pie.

Fabienne: Blueberry pie.

Butch: Well, maybe not that fast, but fast. Okay? Okay?

Fabienne: Okay.

He kisses her once more and heads for the door.

Butch: Bye-bye, sugar pop.

Fabienne: Bye.

Butch: I'm gonna take your Honda.

Fabienne: Okay.

And with that, he's out of the door.

Fabienne sits on the bed and looks at the money he gave her.

And there they are: the classic signs of an abusive relationship. She is bowed, sitting on the floor. She has been deathly afraid of him and flinches at his touch. He kisses her hand and tells her that he's not angry at her, promises her that he'll be back soon. All she can do is apologize and tell him that she's sorry for being so dreadful. It's a brilliant, manipulative sleight of hand that masks the truth: she is not the one who must apologize. His reaction— tyrannical and threatening—would have been disproportionately cruel *no matter what she had done*. This is what abusers are so good at though. They are virtuosos at masking the truth, at making women believe that they deserve it.

"My abuser had brainwashed me into believing that I deserved every bit of the abuse and the terror I went through," said Neha Rastogi of her husband of ten years, Abhishek Gattani.[1] There are recordings of him slapping and verbally abusing her (without which she might not have been believed) in the presence of their two-year-old daughter. They are perhaps most remarkable—and chilling—for the extraordinary calmness in Gattani's voice.

"No, no, no," he says when she tries to explain what a software bug means. "When did I say that's a bug? We talked about bugs right? Is it getting very difficult for you to focus? You really do need help. You need me to take another step and come to you. You need help?"

The sound of a dull *thwack*.

"You don't want to get beaten up?" he asks. "Then control yourself."

I often fantasize about what it would have been like to be a man. I imagine having been born in a tougher, stronger body. I am tall for an Indian woman—5'7"—and when I wear heels, I am as physically imposing as a man. It is an exciting, fire-new feeling. If only I had the broad shoulders to go with it, the musculature . . .

I wonder to myself: would I have been cruel to women? It would be easy for me to dominate women—would I have done it? Just because they were there, and because they were weak, and because I could?

One night, I watch as a spider scuttles around my bathroom. No. I correct myself as I look more closely. It is not a spider but its gentler cousin: a daddy long legs.

I grab the bidet from the wall. I turn the hose on it.

Overwhelmed, it washes up against the wall. I turn off the bidet and watch as the creature struggles back to its feet. Despite the power of the jet spray, it has held on; it is (gamely) surviving.

I turn the spray on it again. It flounders and then goes limp.

I turn it off again.

Still—still a little life in the thing—it twitches in a faint hope—

Half-annoyed, half-amused by this game we are playing, I blast it for a good long while. A whole minute. Perhaps, two. Even three. When I release the bidet, I know what I will see, and I see it: a floating, completely dead daddy long legs. With a judder, it swirls down the bathroom pipe. I stare at the empty bathroom floor for a long time.

I think of Nikki Giovanni's poem, "Allowables":

I killed a spider
Not a murderous brown recluse
Nor even a black widow
And if the truth were told this
Was only a small
Sort of papery spider
Who should have run
When I picked up the book
But she didn't
And she scared me
And I smashed her

I don't think
I'm allowed

To kill something

Because I am

Frightened

It is the question I turn over and over in my mind, this question of what we owe each other—*if* we owe anything. What do the strong owe the softest, the poorest, the most helpless? Do we owe them kindness? Or if (as some have suggested) the world is nothing but a hierarchy of people smashing each other, why should the people on top feel bad about smashing those below? (If that is the way of things.) If the world beats *us* down, who are we allowed to beat up? Anybody on a rung below us? Anybody with less power? If my husband smacks me and I smack my dog, are we being blindly obedient to the natural order of things?

I talk about it to my boyfriend and he shows me a poem he has written, "You Should Never Spit on a Tortoise's Back." He has used spitting on a tortoise's back, for some reason, as a metaphor for arbitrary cruelty. The tortoise would be completely unable to do anything about it; it cannot touch its own back. You have done it for no other reason than that you can do it and have no fear of reprisal.

It is a beautiful poem, and I tell him so. I push aside the half-formed thought that in our relationship he has often been the spitter and I the tortoise.

That is often the way with men and women.

Max died a few years ago. He died when I was in America, so I never saw him at the end. I didn't have to. It is enough for me to know that he lived a long life. Not every dog sees it to thirteen. Not every Indian dog.

I don't know if he was happy. I know that he was well fed, and that he was healthy almost all his life, and that he was loved deeply. I know that after that day, I treated him with as much gentleness as I could manage. I know that he was not hit or hurt because he was small and vulnerable. Some days, that feels like all the grace this sorry world could muster. I pray on these stars it was enough.

V
CULTURE

Some Ways to Disappear Girls in Salem, Tamil Nadu

Nearly 60 percent of girls born in Salem, Tamil Nadu, are killed within three days of being born.[1]

1) The milky sap of the oleander
2) Tobacco juice
3) Strangulation
4) The poisonous milk of the irukkam and kalli weeds
5) Dropping crude husks of paddy into just-born's throats
6) Leaving her to the elements
7) Asphyxiating the baby by placing it beneath a pedestal fan at full blast
8) Feeding hot, spicy chicken soup to the babies
9) Throwing her into a well
10) Drowning
11) Burial
12) Burn her at the stake for being a witch (let this Salem dream of the other one)
13) Kill her, kill her, kill her

Cautionary Tale for Brown Women

Instructions: Teach this story in schools. Teach it as the story of what an ideal Indian woman should be. Make young girls repeat it until they know it by heart.

Teach them that it has a happy ending.

The brown woman had come from over the mountains to the village in the east.

They had the usual curiosity about anyone new. She didn't look like much, they said, and indeed it was true that she was not as pretty as the women of that village. The women of that village were milk-skinned, with large almond eyes and noses. She was thinner than them and her features were irregular.

"I come from the west," she told them. One neighbor laughed.

"Why would you move here?"

"I heard that the winds were kinder," and it was true that their village had rain and sun in equal proportion.

"Tell us about the west," they said, curious for they had heard only rumors. She shook her head.

"The earth is red," she said, "and cracked, and the women carry empty buckets for miles. Some days they manage to fill them—a little bit—and on others, the buckets stay empty. Those days the women cry, and the crying keeps me up all night. You could fill a bucket with their crying, but, of course, salt water is useless."

They shuddered and looked at their own rich earth with pride.

"You are lucky to be here," they said, embracing her. "There's enough water and good fortune," and with that, they welcomed her to the village and the evening feasts.

They grew used to her quickly, to the sight of her tall body wandering in the coconut groves. She lived in a small house that she built herself out of straw and brick. To call it a house would sound grand, as it was more of a hut. She built it with astonishing speed, and after it was done, she hung a hammock from a tree outside.

"It's so I can sleep outside on fine days," she explained. They had never seen a hammock before and they asked her laughingly what the point of a house was if all she needed was a hammock.

"I like to be outside," she said. It was something that she took pride in, to be under the stars and see their comings and goings at night.

"There's nothing special about the stars," said one boy. He was very young and his mother immediately shushed him for speaking like that to an elder.

"On the contrary," she said. "You must know where to look. The path that they carve in the sky tells a story."

"What sort of a story?"

She shrugged her shoulders. "Many different stories. Some are about the rains and some are about the lands that are starving and when the tides will be."

They didn't know what to make of that, but they concluded that it was harmless. Not one of them believed her or even liked her, but they couldn't help admiring her. She had a stout laugh and a very ready hand with plants. In no time, she had coaxed skyward green tender shoots of bamboo and mustard flowers that were sharp and radiant. She fell in easily with the ways of their village and they ate what she cooked with joy and pleasure.

It was a young girl who discovered the secret of the stranger's hair. She had never let it loose like the women of that village but had wound it around her head in a tight braid. One afternoon, a girl who was passing by found her brushing her hair with a smooth piece of stone. She exclaimed: "Why, your hair is long enough to dip into a well!"

It was no such thing, but it was certainly long. It was thick and bristly like a rope, but it was alive, every inch of it. The young girl looked at it longingly.

"It is too unruly for me," said the woman. "I can't do my chores without tying it up."

"I wish I had such hair," sighed the girl. She showed the stranger her hair, which was limp and straggled over one shoulder. "It would be my pride."

"You can have a lock of mine," laughed the older woman. "Here, cut off a piece and clip it into your head, if you like. Then as you go about the fields, you can feel the weight of your hair."

The girl, delighted, did as she said. When she got to her own house, she told her parents and they exclaimed at the thickness of her hair.

Others, hearing this story, went to the little straw house to ask if she could spare more hair. One was a grandmother, one was a coquette, and one was a bald man who had always wanted to look handsome. Saying that her hair would soon grow back, she cut each of them a good hank of her hair from the crown. The grandmother opened her hands to receive it, and then the coquette, blushing and grinning. Finally came the bald man, and when he took the hair, he burst into tears.

When they were gone, she felt the ridges of the hair that was left. Well, it would soon grow back and with that, she retreated to the hammock for the evening.

The rains came, and they cleaned the fields splendidly. Nothing was left of the dirt in the streets when the rains were done. The crops stood in the water, struggling to poke their heads above it, and the earth was waterlogged entirely. It was then that the bald man returned to the stranger, and asked her for a tooth.

"A tooth!" she said in surprise, and he told her that his youngest daughter had fallen from a coconut tree and knocked out one of hers.

"She weeps all day and night without it," said the man as an excuse. The woman thought of those she had left behind in the village in the east and the memory moved her to say yes. The man extracted the tooth carefully with pliers he had brought and thanked her before taking it away.

This story—which the man repeated to everyone—cemented her reputation for good in the village. They said to each other that there was a woman in a small hut who they could go to if they needed anything. The rains had clogged some of the fields and they were worried that they might suffer like the villagers in the east.

"Our son wishes to have your straw and bricks," said one family to the woman. "His fields have suffered and he has nothing to sell. You, we know, can build another house. We are not blessed with such skill. What great fortune it is!"

They were right. The woman willingly pulled down her straw and brick hut. But she did not build another house. From then on, she slept in the hammock regardless of whether or not it was a fine day.

For a while, they were satisfied, and the water receded, and the woman slept alone in her hammock. But then the weather changed again, and this time a glittering wind swept through the village, the kind of wind that troubled the woman.

"It was such a wind as this," said the woman to the others, "that left us poor in the west. There is no water in such a wind— not even a drop. It leaves the earth brackish."

One man was anxious for his family and he asked for the woman's mustard field. Now this was a small patch of field and its flowers were a blazing yellow, the kind of yellow that spoke of good health and radiance. The woman felt a deep reluctance in her heart.

"I have tended to it long," she said. "Water it well." But the man was already digging up the flowers and carrying them away. The woman went to her hammock and counted the stars that were coming out in the sky. She had nothing to wear but a garment of linen; she had given her other clothes to the young women of the village.

"You are older than us," they said, "and we have not so much." They left her hammock with their hands full.

The woman's prediction came true—the wind was a harsh one. It swept over cliffs and grass like a child in a temper, and there was nothing it did not put its hand on. There was no well it did not dry up, no field it did not lay waste to. When the wind was gone, the earth showed its suffering, and the women walked as far as they could to find what was not to be found.

Without water, the fields died and there was not a pot of rice left to be had. The villagers wailed in hunger and they had no choice but to go to the woman.

"I only have a hammock," she said, when she understood their predicament. "I would give you this except that it is precious. I knotted this hammock; I strung together the ropes for hours while

I listened to the crickets in the trees. In its fibers, I feel my dreams breathing."

"We cannot eat or drink a hammock," they said.

"I have nothing," she said, again, before understanding what they meant. She thought and then spoke aloud.

"If I give you this," she said, as if to herself, "you will remember my name. I have wanted to be remembered; I have longed to be loved, to be dear to a people I had been unknown to. That is what I want in the world, there is nothing that I want as much as this. I will give you what you want. Yes, I will give you what you want. It will be an act of love. Done for love, and by it, you shall love me. You will speak of me to your children, to your children's children and the ones who will come after that. I will be beloved in every language and you will think of me when you see a branch of coral or sow the shining fields of mustard. People will come from far and wide, and they will say here is the village of the woman who came from the west. I will give you the last thing I have; I will sacrifice it, and in return, I will live forever."

She lay on the red earth and turned her face up to the stars while they brought the knives.

It was all over in two hours. They gutted her to the bone and ate the soft innards. There was no fighting; there was enough of her for everyone. Every man, woman, and child in the village ate and passed a joint of meat to the other. They roasted her limbs and ate with good appetite. They chewed the tender meat of her heart and cracked the bones to suck the marrow out. They ate her fingernails and washed her eyes down with the last cup of her blood. That night, they slept sounder than they had in some time.

The seasons passed and with them came the rains. Soon, it was as if the village had never been dry. Life returned to normal and the children shouted to each other in the fields. Everybody forgot about the woman and they left the hammock to the corruption of nature. In a year, there was nothing left of it but a few pieces of rope.

Things Indian Women Need to Get Used to Saying

It feels so good to say it, even though I say it so little.

"No. Sorry," I tell a boy who comes up to me, asking if he can talk.

"No?" he says, with an appealingly boyish grin. "No means you're not interested in talking to me?" He is counting on the fact that I won't say those words.

"Yes."

"Oh, you *are* interested in talking to me?"

"No," I say so vehemently that a table full of people turns back to look. "I am not interested."

Actually, that's not how I say it. I snap it out as if I'm a shark biting pieces off him with each bite.

"I! Am! Not! Interested!"

Now I've done it. He looks shocked. Truly and utterly shocked. Before he can say something, I stalk off, feeling a curious mixture of emotions—guilt, worry, nervousness, but mostly, pride.

Homework Assignment #1

Practice until you are familiar with the taste of the following.
Keep them in your mouth and use them liberally

1) No
2) That won't be possible
3) That's inconvenient for me
4) I don't think so
5) You're interrupting me
6) I already said that
7) That's not my problem
8) I'm not interested
9) I can't do that
10) I won't do that
11) I don't have the time
12) I don't have the energy
13) No, thank you

VI
FAILURE

Agnostic

There are things I like about religions although I am agnostic.

I like their sounds. I like the sound of the temple bell ringing, of the azaan in Old Delhi (while the crows stand enraptured). I like the swell of the church organ in the distance (always playing "Für Elise"). I like the chanting of Latin prayer, the hymns and the golden voices of the Boston choirboys. I like the sound of a veena accompanying a devotional Hindi song. I want to hear Sufi music at night in Nizamuddin. I am thrilled by the qawwali and the whirling dervishes of Old Delhi. I hear the chants of the Hindu priests. The Lotus Sutras.

> *asato mā sadgamaya*
> *tamasomā jyotir gamaya*
> *mrityormāamritam gamaya*
> *oṁ śhānti śhānti śhāntiḥ*

I like their scents. The whiff of attar on the old-fashioned pocket squares our grandfathers would carry. I like the sizzle of an incense stick, the scent of jasmine (fresh from the freezer) wound around the portraits of the dead in a Hindu home.

Then there are parts I want to touch and consume so that they become a part of me. The sacred wafer, the communal wine. The charred body and blood of the Redeemer. I like to squat in a graveyard and touch the forbidden tombstones, to run my fingers over the inscriptions in the gathering dusk. I admire the cool, rosy marble of a Muslim tomb or the stone of a Hindu idol carved by loving hands. The sacred architecture of a confessional, of a dome rising high into pink foreign skies.

The signs and symbols of faiths are beautiful to me. A man kissing the ring of the Pope. Another man kissing the feet of a saint. The Muslim man who touches his forehead to his prayer rug. The flames leaping above a body on the burning ghats, or the son who cracks his dead father's skull to let a piece of the soul in. *Amen!*

I am—at best—a tourist in the land of religion. A sightseer with no real skin in the game. My father is a Christian (cheerfully agnostic) and my mother is a Hindu (unwillingly atheist). They say that the child of two religions always adopts the religion of her father's, and so it was with me. In a way. I was baptized, but I knew nothing about it when it was happening. I was a baby being crossed with water while people dubbed me a newly minted member of an arbitrary religion.

The name they picked was Anna—again, a strange choice. I certainly don't feel like an Anna, though it's a nice name. It's rounded and soft—the A seems pure in the mouth. I didn't know it was a typical Syrian Christian name (I knew more Mercys and Arielles than Annas), but I am glad that it is. In another life, I think, I wouldn't have minded being an Anna.

I wasn't raised either Christian or Hindu. Neither fish nor fowl nor good red herring. I went to Sunday school (I hated it) and temples (equally disappointing). When confronted with the truth that I could become anything I wanted, I chose to be a witness. An observer.

This decision was made much easier by the fact that nobody in Kerala seemed to care much about religion. Oh, Christianity had seeped into the state (like "tea from a teabag," said Arundhati Roy) all right, but the world I was exposed to was one of privileged unconcern. It was exemplified in the act of eating beef, that most sacrilegious of things. Unlike the rest of the nation, the Nairs and the Menons and the Vergheses ate their beef ularthiyathu with hanks of porotta.

The Christian school I attended never asked us whether we went to church. They never made us say prayers before class or told us that Jesus loved us. They didn't terrify us with visions of hellfire if we sinned (although they gave us very little opportunity to sin). So I went to school and I came home, and I lived out my days not thinking about God—whether he was Christ or Allah or Vishnu or whoever He was. If there was a man in the sky, He had zero to do with me.

It wasn't until I transferred to Kodaikanal International School (KIS) that G-O-D was shoved down my throat. At KIS—that trendy, sneering school for the wealthy—I learned that God existed. And yes, He was a Christian God. KIS, you see, was built by missionaries. True believers. White people who longed to come to India to convert the heathens, the pagans, the poor brown people. Some of them were like St. John Rivers from *Jane Eyre*. They genuinely wanted to convert the unwashed masses to the Way of the Light (perhaps picturing themselves as a shining white Jesus). The rest were just in it for a free holiday in a cheap country.

We were asked to take basic Christianity for international baccalaureate credit and we had to watch Mel Gibson's overwrought *The Passion of the Christ* (even at sixteen, this movie felt like propaganda).[1] I resented the messaging about God—the constant exhortations to "praise" and "worship" and "be thankful for his infinite mercies!"—that we received at prayer breakfasts.

Silly rabbit. We only went to prayer breakfasts because they served pancakes. Didn't the pastor know that? I marveled at his stupidity.

No, I found nothing Christian in that school, the school that I had to win a scholarship to afford. That school filled with rich kids. ("'Tis easier for the camel to enter through the eye of a needle than it is for a rich man to enter into the Kingdom of Heaven [. . .]") No more incentive to come closer to God. God, as far as I was concerned, was represented in the fluffiness of a golden pancake in a pool of syrup.

It was about then, I think, that I encountered TV evangelists for the first time. I'd been switching channels idly, looking for something in English. And lo and behold, there was she was, this incredibly arresting woman with close-cropped hair in a slightly mannish suit. Banging her fists emphatically on her podium. She didn't just *have* stage presence, she blasted you with hot jets of it. And she asked rhetorical questions. Lots of rhetorical questions.

Unlike the other English TV shows I'd watched, this one wasn't high budget. There was nothing for you to see really, other than this woman thundering away at her podium. And yet it was impossible to be bored or to take one's eyes off her. Much of what she said didn't even make sense—or rather, it didn't matter if it made sense. The words weren't important. What mattered is that they came together in a glorious *gloop* of conviction. She had an unshakeable conviction—the thing that we all longed for.

"YOU ASK YOURSELF, WHAT IS GOD? WHAT IS THAT MYSTICAL, ALL-LOVING, ALL-EMBRACING PRESENCE WHO MOVES IN MYSTERIOUS WAYS? CORINTHIANS TELL US WHAT THESE MIRACLES ARE BUT SO WE KNOW, AND WE ASK OURSELVES, IS THIS THE ANSWER? THE BIBLE TELLS US IN CORINTHIANS 4 THAT WE SHOULD SEEK, AND SEEK, AND THAT HE WILL SHOW US THE WAY, BUT WE DOUBT! WE DOUBT, AND SO WE STRAY,

AND WE TURN AWAY FROM THE PATHS OF GOD THAT HIS SON, THE REDEEMER, THE ONE, THE OMNISCIENT, THE OMNIPOTENT, HOLY TRINITY, THE HERE AND THE HEREAFTER, THE ALPHA, THE OMEGA, HE WHO SHALL RAISE US UP AND CALL US BLESSED IN THE HOUSE OF HIS FATHER . . . JESUS CHRIST!"

She'd nailed it. Ole girl knew. And it was the rest of us (miserable, doubting Thomases and Thomasinas) who slunk around the world not knowing. It was she—the TV evangelist with the toothy smile and the blonde pageboy bob—who knew the secret. Like any salesman, like any door-to-door Jehovah's Witness, she had learned the confidence trick.

It was this kind of woman, I knew instinctively, that had the requisite charisma to convert people to her beliefs. Like the prophet Harold Camping.

Here lies Harold Egbert Camping
Born: July 19, 1921
Died: December 15, 2013 (aged ninety-two)
Occupation: Talk radio personality, self-published Christian author, evangelist
Known for: Christian broadcasting, end-times predictions

Camping was an ordinary man. An unremarkable man, except for the fact that he'd predicted the end of the world unsuccessfully multiple times.[2]

Multiple times! I found myself impressed with his conning ability. Truly, he was Nostradamus.

I could understand he'd gotten away with it the first time. He'd already built up quite a radio following and I could understand that there would be people willing to believe it the first time. (*Oh, my dear Muriel, did you hear what that nice Christian man said on the*

*radio? He said the end of the world was coming! I know . . . I suppose
we'd better go to church this Sunday, after all!*)

Even, perhaps, the second time. (That sweet old preacher
was wrong then but he might be right this time!) But I couldn't
understand how he'd done it a third time. More impressive still,
he'd gotten his followers to quit their jobs, pull their kids out of
school, and move into trailer vans in the desert. All with vague
threats and exhortations to save their damned souls.

"The Rapture," he warned them solemnly, "*is coming*."

The Rapture was an event—according to Camping—that
would distinguish the sinners from those who were to be saved.
If you repented and accepted Christ into your heart,[3] you might
still have time. You'd be raptured up to heaven. If you didn't . . .
well, you'd be left on earth with the rest of the sinners to await the
inevitable, terrible Judgment Day.

That would happen, he predicted, on May 22, 2012. His
radio network—Family Radio—spent $100 million getting that
prophecy out to non-believers. *One hundred million dollars.*[4] To
all the witless, poorly informed Americans who were his targets.
Of course, it would happen in America. Nobody in America
would bother to do basic fact-checking (if they had, they would
have found another of Camping's false predictions dating back to
1993). America was the land of catfishing and credulousness. Of
course, religion was the opium of the masses—what else did they
have besides Big Macs and the myth of American exceptionalism?

From the comfort of my blanket-and-laptop fort, I snicker.
Then it hits me: that could have happened here. In fact, it already
has.

There are things I don't like about religions.

Religions flourish under cruel conditions and nobody can
deny that India is a cruel country. Perhaps, as my mother says
somberly, the cruelest country in the world.

I dispute her hotly on this. I point out every country that is just as bad or worse. Even in the First World, most Americans are tortured, living lonely lives. Paycheck to paycheck. I tell her that they have no healthcare, a racist political system, and a president who is no better than a dictator. They are slipping without knowing it into a fascist future and their children are dying in school shootings. At least we don't have school shootings.

She listens and tells me maybe that is true. But I can see she is not convinced. And—truth be told—sometimes, I agree with her. In this country, we do not have the illusion of equality. You see, if you take a map of Delhi–NCR and drew a straight line beginning from Civil Lines in the north and stopping somewhere around Cyber City, Gurgaon, in the south, you will be able to locate almost everybody who matters on that line.

If you want to know what someone does, what their background is, what their caste is, and the rate at which they pay their taxes, all you have to do is ask, "Where d'you put up?" and, "What do your parents do?" Often the second question is all you need to answer the first. Then, when one gives the answer, they will nod ponderously, looking like nursery schoolteachers when their students spell the alphabet correctly. Then, they will go into a long exegesis that is designed to prove their familiarity with "embassy road."

(*Em-bassy road . . . Yes, yes . . . Haanji. I know where that is. It is after Golf Links. There is a very nice restaurant there . . . Your parents are government officials? Yes, yes. I know many people on embassy road . . . very nice location. Central Delhi and all that. Very close to Khan Market. You know Mrs. Mehra? Very nice lady. She stays on that road . . . I'll introduce you to her . . .*)

In Delhi, the politicians live on Raisina Hill and in the diplomatic enclave in Chanakyapuri. Moneyed artists and students with trust funds live in newly gentrified Hauz Khas Village, where you can buy a complete wedding trousseau if you have 75,000–1,000,000 rupees to spare. Old-money families live in *kothi*s in the colonies: Defence Colony, New Friends Colony, Nizamuddin East (Nizamuddin West was for the nouveau riche). All of them have farmhouses—acres of farmland—in Chhatarpur and apartments in Gurgaon or Noida.

For the moguls, the tycoons, you have to go to Aurangzeb Road in Lutyens' Delhi—a mere two streets away from the prime minister's house at 7 Race Course Road. There are no apartments on Aurangzeb Road, only the enormous bungalows built by Edwin Lutyens in the 1920s.

The British had left, but the men (and a few women) who lived in Lutyens' Delhi were still the rulers of all of India, even though you can never see them. If you drive down Aurangzeb Road or Amrita Shergill Road you will only be able to see high, heavy gates and guards in khaki. Perhaps, if you are lucky, you will glimpse a car swishing through or gardens that look like water. Perhaps, on Sundays, you might see them as they stroll past the tombs in Lodi Garden. But that is all. The only time the rich and the poor are thrown together is at traffic intersections.

A rose costs 10 rupees. A balloon the same. For a moment, when you look at these children, it seems right and natural that girls should have flowers and boys should have balloons with cartoon animals printed on them. But they do not hold it for themselves. Nothing is for themselves.

The children sleep on the streets in the painful heat of summer and in the, much worse, bite of winter. So often they die there, the homeless ones. When the temperature dips that low, they do not have enough rags or enough body fat to keep them alive. (Meanwhile, a woman holds up a drink—buttered rum punch— somewhere in a bungalow in south Delhi and exclaims that winter is the only bearable season in the city.)

Sometimes, they die because a drunk has decided to drive home from one of the posh bars that he frequents. He could easily afford a cab home but why should he not have the pleasure of driving while he is drunk? After all, he is rich. Nothing can happen to him. Even if he loses control, even if he slams his car over their jerking bodies on the pavement, he can plead ignorance of the event. He can pay his servant to take the rap. The police will look the other way despite the plethora of evidence that it was him driving. And he can saunter out of the station to go watch the latest Salman Khan movie.

The children who watch with big dark eyes as another development goes up over their Dharavi slum. They are watching a colossal building being erected, a building with twenty-seven stories. It cuts a ruthless slice of the Bombay skyline; it cannot be ignored for it is the house of Mukesh Ambani, who is worth roughly about $27 billion.

A billion dollars for each story. It's nice. Symmetrical.

What are they thinking, these children? What could they be thinking as they tap dully on our car windows or note our expensive handbags as we brush past them on the pavement? How could they not be filled with a titanic rage? How could they not want to murder us?

Amitav Ghosh describes an encounter he had had with a poor couple in *The Ghosts of Mrs. Gandhi*, who he felt should be angry, but wasn't. Although they had lost all their sons in the Sikh riots and were eking out a precarious existence on about ten feet of space, they were not angry. No fire of revolt rose in them. They merely said: "It is God's will."

God! Ah, here we have the answer. It was God who kept the hungry and the poor from eating the rich. It is God (speaking through such convenient figures as Mata Amritanandamayi or Gurmeet Ram Rahim Singh Insaan)[5] who buoys up the starving and keeps the diseased alive. It is God's men, his godmen, who stride through villages where farmers are committing suicide and tell them the rains will come *if they believe*. You must do whatever it takes (like Gurmeet Ram Rahim, aka the Love Charger, who allegedly convinced 400 men to castrate themselves in order to attain spiritual enlightenment).[6]

Feed the gurus and the godmen money. Make temples for them and throw yourselves down at their altars. Sacrifice your children to tantrics to grow your coffers.

Religion, whisper the irreligious, is the only hope you have.

It is perhaps from this necessity—this promise that religion offers the poor—that the myth has grown that India is a spiritual country. No, this is not a spiritual country. This is a country in which human life is not held especially dear. It is easy to mistake not caring about the flesh for caring about the spirit.

I think of the friend who texted me when he saw pallbearers set down a corpse to pop into the liquor shop (dry day started at 5 p.m., you see, and it wasn't like the corpse was going anywhere on its own).

That could have been any poor person. Any Muslim. Any Dalit. Anybody whose flesh wasn't seen as particularly important to the state.

What did they believe when they were alive? Were they pious?

Now, when I think about it, what do I believe in?

I like churches, I like museums. I want to believe in the irradiance of Christ. I am looking for the cheap salvation that the TV evangelists seem to offer. I would like to have the devoutness of my grandmother when she went on her forty-day milk fast for Vishnu. I do, in so many ways, agree with Yann Martel in *Life of Pi*: "To choose doubt as a philosophy of life is akin to choosing immobility as a means of transportation."

But everything has been too dark for too long. I can feel something that keeps me from belief in an easy way out. I have some sticking places in me, some things that keep me from wandering into the safe arms of religion.

Not everything that is beautiful is safe. Not everything that comforts us is good. In a cruel country, we would do well to strain our eyes to look past what is beautiful. What comforts us. That is why God has not been enough for me. I am filled with doubt.

Counting Black Sheep

I

It is the summer of 2014 and you live in Cambridge, Massachusetts—home to both Harvard University and Massachusetts Institute of Technology. You know that some of the country's finest brains are packed into an area of 7.1 square miles. Cambridge is electric—the kind of place where the kids at the bar are locked in a fierce argument over quantum physics. You walk through the universities and it seems plausible that you will encounter the solution to the Navier-Stokes equations scribbled carelessly on a blackboard.

One day, you're on the T when a lanky kid boards the train, carrying a Rubik's cube. You watch him spin the cube in his fingers as the stations flash by. He turns it with preciseness, his brain visualizing patterns you can't see. Four stops later, he solves it.

II

As a child, you struggle with math and science. Your parents draft an endless number of tuition teachers to help you after school. They are severe as caricatures in a Dickensian novel. One of them—a man you dub "The Pincher"—grabs your arm when he sees you scribbling a wrong value for the length of the hypotenuse. This is your signal that you're making a mistake. If you don't correct yourself, he would twist your arm, giving you a Chinese burn. ("I don't understand," he says, "I just don't *understand* how you can be so slow.") The days you are slow, your arms ache from elbow to wrist.

In a society where proficiency with numbers is paramount, you are not allowed to forget that you are an anomaly. At your school, the students who scored the highest in their exams chose science. These are the future successes: the engineers, the doctors, the kids dreaming of Silicon Valley. (Your cousins, who have all chosen science, are well on their way to becoming neurosurgeons.)

The students who are middling—good, but not excellent—choose commerce. They will be businessmen, have mid-level management jobs in companies. The rest (slackers, losers, the bottom of the class) choose arts. You think seriously about choosing arts.

You know you have to leave.

III

It is 2009 and you are scoring a practice LSAT (Law School Admission Test). Biting your lip, you add the numbers up again, hoping you've made a mistake. You scribble the total at the bottom of the page. No mistake. The numbers glare up at you. *168.*

You are an English major (you had originally planned to major in economics but were forced to make it your minor after you figured how much math was involved in it) in your final year of college. You have decided to go to law school. Law school is a sensible path, you think. Lawyers aren't celebrated in India the same way engineers or doctors are, but it's still a respectable career choice. You will go to Harvard Law, you resolve. Your family knows the name. They respect it. You can't be a neurosurgeon, but you *can* go to Harvard Law.

Except, you can't.

The LSAT is divided into three parts. Logical reasoning, reading comprehension, and analytical reasoning. The raw score in each section counts towards your scaled score out of 180.

Logical reasoning is easy enough for you. It consists of finding errors in arguments. Picking the statement that strengthens the argument.

Reading comprehension is easier still. It is lit-crit lite. It's nothing on your Milton seminar and you regularly race through that section with ten minutes to spare.

Analytical reasoning is the problem(s). In the LSAT, there is a particular type of question that appears in this section, known as a logic game. You have eight and a half minutes to finish each logic game. (Like the puzzle Hermione solves to find the Philosopher's Stone.) The typical logic game goes something like this:

An athlete has six trophies to place on an empty three-shelf display case. The six trophies are bowling trophies F, G, and H and tennis trophies J, K, and L. The three shelves of the display case are labeled 1 to 3 from top to bottom. Any of the shelves can remain empty. The athlete's placement of trophies must conform to the following conditions:

1) J and L cannot be on the same shelf.

2) F must be on the shelf immediately above the shelf that L is on.

3) No single shelf can hold all three bowling trophies.

4) K cannot be on shelf 2.

You hate them. It's hard to describe why. They don't even require any advanced mathematical skill. They are just problems, but you're no good at solving problems.

To get into Harvard Law, you need an LSAT score of at least 175. A full seven points above where you are currently. It doesn't matter how many practice tests you take or how much better you get at the other sections, you panic at the logic games. You cannot solve logic games fast enough, which means you have zero chance at ever scoring a 175. *That* is the one number you are sure of.

You crumple up the test and throw it across the room. *Elle Woods is a lie*, you think. You rest your head on your arms.

IV

You go to another law school. There are other law schools besides Harvard. When people ask, you tell them you're going to law school in Boston. They get excited because they assume you mean Harvard. Where else would a desi kid go?

V

In one of those weird coincidences poets love, you start dating a desi boy who goes to Harvard Law. He's an engineer, good at problem-solving. He thinks you're cool—funny, sweet, pretty. He doesn't think you're very smart. It takes you a while to figure this out (of course he doesn't *say* it) but you can tell from the little things. Like when you tell him you're applying for an internship in New York and the only thing he says is, *well, that's a really difficult internship to get,* even though you hadn't asked him about your chances, you'd only been telling him how excited you were to apply.

You throw away the application.

VI

One day, you're struggling to split the bill in a café. It's not a hard bill. Math anybody should be able to do in their head, but you can't seem to do it. "You're the worst Indian ever, huh?" says the waiter jokingly. You say, "Yes."

VII

It is the summer of 2014 and you are depressed. You don't *know* that you are depressed; you think depression is something dramatic. Something other people have. What you have is something quiet, much more subdued. It is simply that you don't want to wake up in the mornings, because you're on a fellowship and can't find a full-time job. (Maybe you didn't look hard enough, but either way, it's your fault.) Because you didn't graduate with honors. Because your visa is about to expire, and because you aren't getting sponsored by any employers, and because you'll have to go back home if something doesn't change immediately.

This isn't something that should happen to an Indian, you think. This doesn't make sense. You only hear about Indians succeeding.

* * *

In 2011, a woman named Amy Chua wrote a book about how the Chinese parenting style was superior to the Western one. The book—which instantly became a smash hit—was named *Battle Hymn of the Tiger Mother*. In it, she recounts how she raised her daughter to master the piano by calling her "garbage" and threatening to withhold food and burn toys if she didn't play the piece perfectly.

As I read that particular anecdote, I thought of the mathematics tutor I'd had at age eleven, "The Pincher." Whenever I came up with the wrong answer or didn't know how to proceed, he would take my arm and twist the delicate skin of my wrist between his fingers like dough. The pain, although uncomfortable, was low-grade. It was bearable. What upset me was his expression: completely devoid of any emotion, only an eerie calm. He was not punishing me because he *enjoyed* it, I think. There was no sadism in him in those moments. I think he was punishing me because that was routine. That was what was expected of him and of me.

Chua's example of a "tiger mom" (a strict disciplinarian who does not believe in prioritizing the self-esteem of a child) is not unique to China. All over India, there are tiger moms, tiger dads, tiger tutors. They are the ones taking away their children's playtime, the ones waiting anxiously for each progress report from school, the ones who stay up to check their children's homework or to drop in on their neighbors to ask questions about how *their* child is doing. ("Not as good as Sushila? Sushila is the class topper, of course.")

"No," said K's mother when she heard what I was asking. K was a girl in my class who I'd never seen outside of school but I'd wanted to invite her to my birthday party. It was to be a modest affair, only the girls in my class, but we would have cake, plates of finger food and K studied so hard—so consistently hard—that I wondered what it was like for her to have fun. It struck me that I had never seen her face relax or soften in a laugh. It was always so serious and intense, always focused on the notebook in front of her.

"It'll only be for an hour or two and there aren't any exams coming up," said my mother. She looked expectantly at the other woman. Asking for an hour or two of a twelve-year-old's time on a Saturday afternoon didn't seem ludicrous, but J's mother stared at us as if it was.

"She'll be busy. Studying." With that, the door closed—softly, but with a firm *click*—in our faces.

I don't remember what happened to K and it feels silly to record that I have pity for her. Wherever she is, she has little need for my pity. She probably came first in the board examinations and became a doctor. Or an engineer. But that is the abiding image I have of her, the only memory: one of a little girl who couldn't come to a birthday party on a Saturday afternoon because she was busy studying.

It is our culture, that's all. That's all that is said about it. We produce excellence, roars a man who's speaking at a South Asian legal conference in New York. I sip my coffee as he points out that Indians in America are a model minority. "Look at the contributions we made to the world, whether it's at home or abroad. We can do this . . . because we have a history of pushing ourselves to excel."

He's not wrong, I think. In America, one of the first things I note is the extraordinary permissiveness of parents. It is the first time I have heard a girl swear into the phone, cussing at her mother, "You bitch!" It is the first time I have seen young men and women work so little, study such meager amounts. On my college campus, as I see people stumbling hungover to class—still in their clothes from last night—I wonder if everybody is there for some larger purpose that I have missed, some promise of enjoyment that was not conveyed to me.

The clothes girls are permitted to wear, the fact that dating itself is permitted—it all approximates parody. I watch the movie *Mean Girls*, in which a mother opens a door, sees her teenage daughter rutting with a boy, and says, "Let me know if you need anything. Some snacks? A condom?" I think, *but that's just American culture, isn't it?* We don't let our kids waste their time dating. That's why we have the Periodic Table memorized, we tell ourselves, while the average adult American can barely do a math problem. *Their* tutors don't pinch and are therefore inferior.

This perceived superiority in culture is what Indians in the diaspora point to over and over again. In her memoir, Mindy Kaling writes ruefully of the time she won an honorary prize at a summer camp when she was a kid. "My parents took it away," she says, "and explained to me that it wasn't a real prize." She credits this with shaping her to some degree because it made her hungrier for success than she might otherwise have been. And indeed, looking at her meteoric rise—the first South Asian woman to be an American showrunner—you can imagine this is true. If you put enough pressure on coal, you get—what? Diamonds. It is the promise of becoming a diamond that sustains us, that feeds our children. We tell them stories of Indra Nooyi and Sundar Pichai. This is how far you can go. If only you can run fast. You could be something special, couldn't you?

About a month ago, I did stand-up comedy, which I'm relatively new to. It was an all-women line-up and I walked around the room, telling jokes about being an artist in India. There was one joke in particular that I wanted to make, but it was too dark, I thought. The energy was too sweet, too cheery to risk denting. I hesitated for a moment. Then I moved on to the next joke.

"What happened when the son told his father, "Papa, I want to become an artist'?"

No. Too dark.

When I tell people I'm a writer, I am accustomed to hearing certain responses. If I'm telling a man that I write, there is, of course, the patronizing reply, "Oh, lovely! Have you published anything yet?" There is the more outrageous "a writer? If you don't mind me asking, how do you pay rent?" And then there is the worst comment of all. "You're so brave for pursuing this." I find it astonishing that people call me brave for doing something I really, truly, want to do. Would they call me brave for eating a muffin or for watching a TV show I like?

And yet, I understand the comment. Art is precarious in our society—anybody who occupies the position of an *artist* is at once thrilling and dangerous. If you're not a doctor, or an engineer, or a lawyer, or an investment banker (and these last two professions are still new to the list of *acceptable professions for brown people*), you are a renegade, a maverick, an absolute madman. When you have a path so clearly marked out for you, why would you venture into strange territory? Why would you want to break a path through a hedge when the main road is right there?

A friend of my mother's remarks over dinner, "Have you heard of style bloggers? My goodness, this generation is certainly wonderful. The professions that you come up with and create!"

Food vloggers, style bloggers, YouTube makeup gurus, Instagram influencers, lifestyle experts, stand-up comics, and content creators—there is no end to the number of professions that millennials have designed for themselves. And yet, so few, so very few of those professions are taken up by Indians. Comedy collectives like East India Comedy (which has millions of subscribers) or entertainers like Lilly Singh are not what the average Indian dreams of becoming. For the average Indian, getting into the IITs are a dream.

Often referred to as the most competitive test in the world, the admission test for the Indian Institutes of Technology (the Joint Entrance Examination or JEE) is what breaks people. There are only 10,000 spots and nearly half a million students competed for them in 2012. That's an admissions rate of about 2 percent—less than half of the acceptance rate at Harvard, MIT, or Stanford. It is this devastating fact that drives students to work incredibly hard—they spend more than two years learning the science and mathematics tested in the exam. Parents who can't afford tutors take loans or sell their land to send their children to special coaching centers. It's not uncommon for a student to wake up before 4 A.M. to squeeze in additional study time before school begins—in fact, that's the least that's expected of a student preparing for the JEEs.

The test is the only criterion of admission. If you are trying to get into an IIT (and God help you if you are), the only thing you need to "crack," in desi parlance, is the JEE. You can throw away your high-school report cards, your list of extracurriculars, the essay you wrote about grief at the death of a parent. None of those are relevant. In one way, this is excellent: it permits students from poor or disadvantaged backgrounds a fair shot. But it also reflects the painfully narrow nature of Indian education. The only thing that matters is how well you can answer certain questions on certain subjects within a limited time frame. How many hours you can study each day. For years.

It's an extraordinary level of commitment. It is the kind of commitment that you require in order to become a Beyoncé or an Usain Bolt. You are giving up everything else. You are agreeing to consign any hope for a normal life, for things outside work. And yet, you are *not* a Beyoncé or an Usain Bolt. Everyone who works hard to become global superstars—entertainers, athletes, etc.—runs on passion. It is the only fuel that can truly sustain you for a marathon such as that. How can one expect a fifteen-year-old boy who wants to be a frontman in a band to be equally, if not more, passionate about cracking the JEE?

Have you ever wondered what happens to the leftover chocolate in a factory that makes chocolate biscuits? Those pieces in between the giant, gleaming discs stamped by an indifferent machine? Are they gathered together and fed back into the machine? Or are they thrown away?

In May 2017, a fourth-year engineering student from Kerala hung himself in his hostel room at IIT Kharagpur. The student—

his name was Nipun N.—was depressed, according to sources, and unable to cope. It was the second death at IIT Kharagpur in as many months. In April, the body of another student had been found beside the railway tracks. The authorities said that Sana Shreeraj had been suffering from depression. The month before that, a student in IIT Delhi jumped off the fourth floor of a hostel in IIT Delhi. The police said that Nitish Kumar Purti had been suffering from depression and was unable to cope. In the same month, a final-year engineering student of NIT Warangal in Telangana jumped to his death from the fifth floor of his hostel building. There was no suicide note, but his father told the police that he, too, had been suffering from depression. His name was Sanketh Kumar Suryavamsi.

I sit late at night, clicking on headline after headline. The only light in the room is from the soft glow of my computer screen. I type different strings of keywords.

"Student suicide"

"IIT student mysterious deaths"

"Hanging student"

"Students who jumped off buildings"

"Engineering student deaths"

"Suicide notes"

It strikes me how different these deaths are from the ones I have heard about in America or the UK. When a teenager takes too many pills, arranges herself neatly in a car with the fumes on, slits her wrists in the bathtub, decides to shoot up his school, there is a reason. (In the case of a school shooting, there is a 141-page manifesto laying out exactly why.) There is almost always a suicide note. The papers obsess over the *why* for weeks, if not months. They may not always find out, but they put forward every possible explanation they can think of.

I'm watching a show on Netflix called *13 Reasons Why*. I'm watching it out of curiosity, mostly. It is immensely popular—a runaway hit. It was the second most-viewed series on Netflix in the month after it released.

I do not particularly admire the show but I can understand its appeal. It is a show about a once vivacious and outgoing girl, Hannah Baker, who is driven to kill herself because of the actions of the people in her life. In a particularly ghoulish form of revenge, she leaves them tapes to listen to after she dies, in which she enumerates the reasons for her suicide. She says to each offender passionately: "Welcome to your tape." To the boy who spread rumors about her. To the boy who raped her. To the teacher who didn't believe her. They are all guilty and they must take the blame, and they *do*—over thirteen hour-long episodes. By the end of the season—an exhausting, emotionally wearying season—we feel minutely acquainted with Hannah's grievances. Her list of wounds.

So, why are brown children silent? Who do they have to talk to? Not therapists. *Kids in our culture don't need therapy*, somebody tells me when I bring it up. That's a Western notion. Like lactose intolerance or disobeying your parents. Depression is a phantom ailment, after all, one that can be cured with studying. (Perhaps some light exercise that won't interfere too much with studying.) How it is a phantom ailment and still strong enough to kill our children in scores each year is never explained.

Some of them tried to talk. If not in life, in death. One final retort to the void (a teenager who couldn't resist being sassy one last time). There are *some* suicide notes. Some even leave a video. A girl takes to Instagram to write a suicide note filled with emojis, a note that would be adorably childish if it wasn't a suicide note.

One girl—seventeen-year-old Kriti Tripathi of Ghaziabad—wrote a letter to the people in her life. I read it in her handwriting online, where it has been made available for reasons that are unclear to me. It is one of the few detailed accounts I can find of a student's mental state before they committed suicide. It explains much more than most of the stark headlines I read in the newspapers.

First, she writes to her mother with painful lucidity, begging her not to manipulate her younger sister the way Kriti had been manipulated:

"You manipulated me as a kid to like science [. . .] *I took science to make you happy* [. . .] *I still love writing, English, history* [. . .] *and they are capable of exciting me in the darkest times* [. . .]*"*

To her sister, she wrote: *"Do only what you love."* Only, said Kriti, what you love brings happiness and that is the only thing you can excel in.

It strikes me that Kriti's handwriting is perfect. Immaculate, easy-to-read cursive, of the kind we are all taught in Indian schools. She writes well, with ease and fluency. I can see why she loves writing.

I skip over the sections of the letter where she addresses her friends, speaking of them in loving tones. I cannot bear it and those words do not seem to be meant for public eyes. Instead, I read the final paragraph of the letter. It is addressed simply to the government, in a seventeen-year-old's characteristic language:

"Please Government of India, HRD, do something about these coaching institutes. They suck and should be shut down as soon as possible."

She had been in Kota, the town famous for its IIT coaching institutes, for two years.

I am lucky. I have been lucky. My story has a happy ending. If you're wondering why I'm writing this, who the cruel adult was who put pressure on me, I can answer this question for you immediately: no one.

It is perhaps easier to tell you what I do not have than what I have. I do not have schizophrenia. I do not have learning difficulties. I do not have ADHD or chronic fatigue syndrome. I'm not on the spectrum. I do not have bipolar disorder or paranoid delusions. I am not particularly prone to depression—at least, not more than the average person. I have never seriously attempted to commit suicide. (A couple of cutting episodes in college, but that's about it.) My brain is whole and its pathways are lighted clearly. Things work correctly, at least for now. My neurons flare and send signals to each other: each is desperate to keep living. I'm a writer and I have a full-time career. It didn't matter that I couldn't fit into law; I found another way.

Even in my most tender, rawest years, teenage years where I took everything seriously and had no sense of perspective, I was lucky. Even in my failures, I was lucky. When I did poorly in tests, I worried about telling my parents—but not too much, never too much. Somewhere in my subconscious was the dazzling and unshakable belief that this was not the end of the world. *If I failed, it was not the end of the world.* Even when I couldn't get into Harvard, even while I was depressed in Boston, I never thought it was the end of the world.

VII
JUDGMENT

The Aunty Problem

When I talk to my childless friends in America, they often tell me that they can't wait to be aunts. "I'm going to be the cool aunt," they tell me. "Aunts are the ones who bring all the presents but never have any of the responsibilities. Everybody loves aunts!"

Mm-hmm.

Here is the problem: aunts are not the same as aunties.

I spent my childhood in a city in Kerala, the southernmost state of India. Technically, it was the capital of the state, but it might as well have been a village. It was the sort of place where the video store rental guy phones you at 6 P.M. on a Friday night to let you know that he *just* got—in 2002!—a bootleg CD of the 1997 movie *Anastasia*. (You would then race to the store to get it before somebody else checked it out.)

I knew the names of all the neighboring aunties, who were on dropping-by-unannounced terms—perhaps the worst thing in the world to a sensitive teenager. This is how the conversations usually went:

Aunty X: Well, Priya, your skin seems to have got a little spottier.

Aunty Y: *Much* spottier.

Aunty X: And how was your math test? You know, I ran into your math teacher the other day at the bus stop and she said you were really struggling. I can give you the name of a good tuition teacher, the one my daughter goes to, for example . . . and she's first in her class . . .

Aunty Y: I'll make my special cream for your skin. Works wonders.

Aunty X, *triumphantly*: Yes, now that I look at it, it's distinctly spottier.

I didn't quite understand who these women were or why they were allowed to be so rude to me. I somehow imbibed the knowledge—by osmosis?—that I had to call them all aunty regardless of whether we had any blood relationship. I never knew their names but that didn't matter. They looked the same to me.

The thing I hated the most about aunties was that they were the polar opposite of people I'd seen on American TV. People on American TV were always taking three trains and a bus and a brief car ride across the city for a face-to-face encounter that lasted three minutes.[1] In sharp contradistinction, aunties from next door were always popping over for a visit that lasted three hours or longer and took place—as far as I could see—*for no purpose whatsoever*.

Aunty M, *eating murukku, the one snack my Tamil mother always kept in the house*: Gained some weight, haven't you, since the last time I saw you?

Aunty N: You have to cut down on your rice. I read an article about how rice causes you to gain weight.

Aunty M, *handing Auntie N another samosa*: I thought that was chapati.

Aunty N: No, rice.

At this point, they would turn to look at me, as if I had a granary's worth of rice before me. This was always a process I resented deeply, especially because the aunties had visible stomach rolls underneath their saris. It was fascinating to me, that flesh;

it looked almost . . . comfortable. It wasn't going anywhere in a hurry.

And neither were they. It was only at 7 p.m. (decent people's supper time) that either of the aunties made a reluctant move towards the door. Another fifteen minutes of dithering and doorstep conversations, and I could finally unclench.

My mother would laugh at how put off I would be. "You were just the same as a baby," she would say. "If any stranger ever came to the house, you dove under the bed like a seal and refused to come out until they'd gone."

I didn't see why I couldn't do the same well into adulthood.

In order to cope with the constant influx of aunties, I read old books about kings who would sprinkle their moats with sharks to keep people out. After contemplating the cost of a moat and drawbridge, I decided to do something only slightly less expensive: go abroad. America, I reasoned, was on the other side of the globe from India, which meant that I would be as far away as possible from all aunties.

When I announced this plan to my father, he produced a list of suitable American colleges for me. I looked at the first three names on the list. Bryn Mawr, Wellesley, and Mount Holyoke.

"Why are these *all girls'* colleges?"

"They're the best colleges in America . . . I did a lot of research . . . "

"What did you research? 'Best colleges without boys in America'?"

"Honestly," said my dad (the smoothest liar on three continents), "I didn't even *notice* that they were only girls' colleges."

America was a blessing. A haven of calm to me, where people were entirely and completely unconcerned with what I was doing (for the most part). There were no aunties to interfere with me, but I still heard stories.

"Don't put any pictures of yourself doing . . . questionable things on social media," warned a desi acquaintance. "It happened to my cousin. He had a Facebook picture with a boy who was smoking a joint and he"—lowering her voice impressively—"*had to leave school and go straight back to Pakistan*. All because he was in the same room as someone smoking a joint!"

"Well," I pointed out. "Maybe he shouldn't have added them on Facebook. I don't have any of *my* relatives on Facebook."

She laughed derisively. "Of course, he didn't add them! They just . . . found out somehow."

"*How?* Did he have his pictures set to public?" I was paranoid now. I couldn't remember what my social media settings were.

"I don't know how. Maybe they made a fake account and friended him? They have *ways of finding out things*."

This I was inclined to believe. I'd had my own personal experience with the CIA-level investigative skills of aunties in India. One day, when I was craving a cigarette, I snuck out of the house in the afternoon and went to a completely deserted field.[2] Once there, I took further precautions: I found an enormous rock and squatted behind it. When I was sure that absolutely nobody except God could see me, I smoked a cigarette in a hasty fashion. I buried the butt in a shallow grave and scurried home to take a bath and dispose of any olfactory evidence.

The next day, my mother told me: "DON'T smoke cigarettes while you're here."

After that, I'd resigned myself to the fact that I wouldn't be able to do anything secretly. If the aunties had found me out despite my precautions, they were capable of anything. The Aunty Scandal Network ranged far and wide and I had no hope of escaping it. I envisioned my whole life as a series of phone calls from "concerned aunties."

That was what really galled me. The faux concern from the auntiyon. They always framed their snitching as if it came from a place of love, when it was pure, undiluted judgment.

There are cool aunts who bring you food and wine at Christmas. Who teach you how to use lipstick as blush and rub it into the apples of your cheeks as you stand there wondering. There are aunts who joke with you about boys as you get older; the aunts who you suspect have fascinating sex lives themselves. In books and American movies, aunts even take you to buy condoms or help you get on the Pill. But those are aunts. Never aunties.

Aunties, who have long relinquished the pretence of social life, glom on to yours. In vampiric fashion. Sometimes when I think about this, I have faint glimmers of sympathy for them. I imagine them, young and cool, strolling through Bandra or Khan Market or Brigade Road, swinging handbags. I imagine them slowly growing bored, their eyes glazing over with indifference because they have no jobs. I imagine them meeting for lunch only to say, "Yeah, I got another handbag today, so nice, see, see." I imagine them aging rapidly until they have nothing left to do but pick over the bones of other people's gossip.

Perhaps, they seem actively invested in keeping young girls down because they were kept down. And they oppress young women (never men) because they were oppressed. Shut in. Subjected to double standards. Scrutinized and shamed until they internalized the lessons of Indian patriarchy.

When I think of it, I confess I have sympathy. Perhaps aunties know no other way to be. I can have sympathy for them while also decrying their devilish works. I'm human. I contain multitudes and I'm calling it: no longer will we tolerate the tyranny of aunties. "FUCK OFF, AUNTIES." In the words of the Pink Floyd song—*leave us girls alone.*

Homely

Mrs. Bhamra: Which family will want a daughter-in-law who can kick a football all day but can't make round chapatis?
—*Bend It Like Beckham*

Of every single word in the dictionary, the one I hate the most (it's not *moist* or *panties*) is "homely."

(The second is *hubby*. This makes it very difficult for me to read matrimonial columns where the two intersect in nauseating ways.)

The first time I saw the word "homely" was, I think, in L.M. Montgomery's *Anne of Green Gables*. Anne, a frightened twelve-year-old orphan, is described as "homely" because she's skinny and has red hair. From Anne's indignation, I understood that homely meant ugly or plain.

Iyer, 29/165 be of traditional family in search of fair, extremely good-looking, innocent, homely Iyer girl only. 044-23412147

Christian boy, wheatish complexion, 34, divorced, no issue, seeks unmarried Syrian Christian girl, extremely fair and beautiful. Homely girls only.

30 y/o NRI with MBA degree in search of well-educated, fair and beautiful, homely, simple girl. Green card holder misra_pkrajiv@yahoo.co.in.

Not in the Indian context. Homely apparently meant a girl who was *comfortable at home*.[1] Cooking, cleaning, washing dishes, and sewing blouse pieces. Thriftily repurposing leftover ragi to make fresh chapatis. Knowing how to make round chapatis (the *Bend It Like Beckham* struggle.) Other cultures might call it being a domestic goddess a la Nigella Lawson, but in India, it's just being homely.

Homely represents a kind of simplicity to Indian men. An unwillingness to demand things of men, of anyone. (One man tells me that he wants to marry a girl "from the village" because, at least, she'll be simple.) In Bollywood movies, homely women are the ones played by the heroines. Their charms may be overlooked by the hero at first (he's always being distracted by some vixen on a Vespa in Europe), but in the end, she always triumphs.[2]

After going through dozens of marriage classifieds, I concluded that it was the second most desirable trait for Indian women (beaten only by "extremely fair"). Indian men were absolutely *gagging* for homely women.

Indian men! They want so many things, don't they? Here is a comprehensive (but not exhaustive) list of things that Indian men seem to want in a wife:

1) A luminous, pale-skinned beauty, reminiscent of the moon in *The Arabian Nights*. Failing that, a judicious mixture of Aishwarya Rai and Madhubala's features. NB: When it comes to body type, Indian men are divided.

Some have been swayed by the more modern trend of size zero Bollywood actresses. The rest insist upon a voluptuous (but not too much) woman of medium height.

2) A BA/MA/MBA/LLB/PhD degree. This seems to be purely for ornamental purposes since most Indian men are uncomfortable with their wives working.[3]

3) A cooking ability to rival their mothers' (but which will never quite exceed it).

4) An endless wellspring of care, love, and attention (which we can call maternal instinct since Indian men wish to be mothered from the cradle to the grave).

It is no easy thing, this maternal instinct. It requires a woman to wake up between 4 A.M. and 5 A.M. and pack lunches for her husband and children (neat plastic bags of sambar, squared-off sandwiches with pickle and green chutney as demonstrations of love). It requires her to float cheerfully through her day, placating and providing for any in-law or aged grandparents who happen to live in the house. Finally, it requires her to have dinner waiting for her husband the moment he returns home (while having the hot bath drawn, the slippers, and the massage oil waiting for his feet). Whether or not she has just returned from the office herself, she must see to her husband's needs when he gets home. And then to everybody else's. (Before she sleeps, the exhausted doyenne of the house may presumably see to her own.)

5) A suitably upper-class background, with no mad or (worse) poor relatives.

6) A lack of desire to go out (must greatly prefer being at home to going out).

I heard of a man who met his future wife at the bar. Once they got married, he forbade her from going out with him. I would laugh at his hypocrisy were it not so painfully common.

How did I do on this scale? A shabby 1/6.

I have an academic degree and that is about it. I am fair-skinned but not at all Madhubala-like. I am a religious mongrel, a weird mixture of Christian and Hindu atheism. At least two of my uncles were mad.[4] My maternal instinct is so emaciated that it is practically dead. I love going out. *I can't cook.* And I don't want to learn.

Like everybody else, I enjoy watching cooking shows. I enjoy watching Nigella Lawson mouth "that clatter of chocolate chips" as she heaps cream sexily on a meringue. There is something beautiful about the way in which *Top Chef* contestants dribble raspberry coulis on perfectly clean plates. But me, personally? Me, cook?

I tell people that not cooking is a feminist act.

The truth is, I don't particularly like to cook. There are aspects of it—certain rituals—that are pleasing to me. Wiping down a kitchen knife with a soft towel, for instance. Stirring cake mix. Pinching off pieces of dough, rolling them around my fingers. Slicing beans and splitting peas. These are exceptions. Small things that I enjoy doing from time to time, but I do not like to cook.

If you are a '90s kid who was raised on *Friends* reruns like I was, you were cruelly tricked into believing cooking is simple. Cooking looks to you like a stylish working woman who sautés vegetables in a wine reduction while Sade plays in the background. The entire process takes about five minutes and is soothing and cathartic.

When I first moved to America, I saw how easy cooking could be for white people. I stood in their grocery stores and marveled at how everything came in containers—from cartons of egg whites to pre-cooked fish—and thought to myself, *this makes sense.* There was beauty and simplicity to one-ingredient meals, to shake 'n bake chicken and instant pizza. I stood in front of strangely lit freezers in the local grocery store and 7/11 and picked out Lean Cuisines for the nights I was too fatigued from law school to think of cooking.

The American kitchens I went to were simple and their fridges uncomplicated. They stocked a couple of spices, not more. Their meats had a dash of salt and pepper, their spaghetti was cooked in white wine, and the more adventurous ones kept a few bottles of hot sauce on hand. The meal itself, when it was done, was mild and clean and buttery, to suit a baby's palate. A good scrubbing later, voilà! The pot was clean again.

That's *not* Indian food. Indian food is fiddly. Indian food requires several steps. Indian food is exacting. Indian food requires several hours of prep (usually in a hot, fan-less kitchen). Indian food has a billion ingredients—each of which must be purchased in different markets. (Even the simplest meal in the cookbook assumes that you have at least twenty-three–twenty-seven spices in your pantry.) Indian food leaves dishes (and your nails) permanently marked with mysterious yellow stains.

I grew up in a household of complicated dinners. My mother is a Tamil Brahmin and my father a Syrian Christian, which means that I have inherited two distinctly different culinary traditions. (The only thing they have in common is that they require a cupboard full of spices.) I remember that each meal took hours to cook and required a variety of ingredients that had to be purchased from several different markets on Sunday. By the time everything was ready—the tamarind paste prepared, the masala mix put together, the accompanying pickles set out—the dirty dishes were stacked to the ceiling.

The men ate first. My grandfather before my grandmother, always. My grandmothers didn't sit while their husbands were eating: they stood behind them or on the side, serving them another fresh dollop of yogurt, the hottest chapatis, the biggest piece of aloo studded with peppercorns. Although they had maidservants in the house, they supervised everything that went on in the kitchens. (I have no memory of seeing the men in the kitchen, ever.)

When my father married my mother, he adapted to her purely vegetarian diet. The only times he ate meat were when his mother sent over carefully wrapped parcels of fish.

Even after all the trouble spent on making Indian food, the men complain about it. They peer at the six, seven, eight dishes on the table and open their mouths to complain.

"I don't like karela."

"Fish again? Why not some proper meat for a change? Every day you serve the same thing ... "

"Where is the achaar?"

"I thought I asked you to make fresh yogurt. There's never any in the fridge."

"But ... "

"I ... "

"Don't ... "

"Like ... "

"This."

My father, bless his soul, is not a particular man. He grew up eating the burnt crusts of apple pies, the tiny blackened fish my grandmother sent over. There was never any complaint about what was being served or what temperature it was being served at. As long as there was a bottle of hot sauce or chili powder, he was happy as he could be. If he was ever subjected to a government dinner or fancy banquet, he would be sure to come home and stand in front of the fridge, absentmindedly breaking off bits of a loaf of bread and dipping them into a jar of tomato pickle. I had no idea that other men weren't like him.

I had my first inkling of this truth the day my friend's father dropped by our house. He was waiting for us to rehearse some lines we were doing for a school play and said he would be quite comfortable in the drawing room.

"I'd like some ice water," he said pointedly. It was a hot day in Delhi and I felt immediately embarrassed by my omission. I should have asked if he wanted anything.

"I'll get you a glass with ice cubes," I promised him and rushed off. When I came back with two glasses on a tray, he was going through the magazines on the coffee table with an air of superiority.

"What else do you have?"

I was bewildered. It didn't strike me that he meant *what do you have to eat*. It was 3 P.M.; too soon after lunch hour to snack. Even by the most gluttonous Punjabi standards.

"You don't have anything in the fridge? Fresh fruit?"

"Oh." The penny dropped. "I think we have some mango slices."

I came back with a bowl of them. It was a thing of beauty, that freshly sliced mango—maddeningly cool-looking. I longed to eat it myself, even though I wasn't hungry.

I held the bowl out before him, expecting him to take it from me.

"No, no, no, no, no, no," he said irritably. "It needs to be cut smaller. Why is it like this?"

He stabbed at a piece of mango with his fork. My arms were aching but he wouldn't take the bowl from me. He was absorbed in this small, faulty bowl of fruit.

"You didn't learn how to treat guests in your house?"

Standing there, flushed red, humiliated, I thought of flinging the entire bowl at him. It would be a waste of good mango but he deserved to have his shirt ruined with its sticky juice and its sloppy insides.

He was wagging his finger now. I stared at him, at the movement he repeated as patronizingly as if I were a dog.

I wanted to scream at him to fetch it himself, to cut it himself since he had such particular tastes.

I said nothing. I fetched it for him. Just as women usually do for the uncles, the brothers, the cousins, the sons who expect to be waited upon by women all their lives.

* * *

There's a story that one of the most powerful women in the world, Indra Nooyi, likes to tell reporters. When she was named president of PepsiCo in 2001, she came home to tell her family the news. Her mother replied: "You need to go get some milk. We're out."

It was 10 P.M. Indra replied: "Raj [her husband] is home, why don't you ask him to buy the milk?"

Her mother said: "He is tired."

An upset Indra went out, got the milk, drove home, and banged it down on the kitchen table. "Tell me, why do I have to buy the milk and not somebody else?"

Her mother looked at her (Indra says it was a look she never forgot) and said, "When you pull into the garage, leave the crown there. Don't walk in with it because you are first a wife and a mother. And if the family needs milk, you go get the milk. That is your primary role in life."

When I read this story, I didn't perceive it as Indra did—a tale about where your real value lies. It wasn't a heart-warming reminder of the importance of family but a painful one. *Look, you are first a wife and mother.* Even if you crawl your way out of the middle-class suburbs to become *the first female president of Pepsi,* even if you have a net worth that runs into $150 million, even if it's 10 P.M. and you're exhausted from a long day of doing business with the most powerful men in the world, *you still have to go and fetch the milk.*

We, Indian women, take particular pride in looking after men. Don't we? I think of this as I hear housewives boast, "Oh, I went away for two weeks to visit my sister-in-law and Kumar lost fifteen pounds! It's so sad, I don't know how he would manage to feed himself if I wasn't around! And you should have seen the state of the bedroom . . . clothes everywhere, and all this with a daily maid. It was chaos, I tell you . . . "

I think of this as I read an article in which an Indian man laments his singledom. "I have no place in the village, as a single man. If I was married, my wife could cook for me, make tea, tell me when to take a bath . . . "

Jhumpa Lahiri describes this particular phenomenon in her breakout collection, *Interpreter of Maladies*. The protagonist in the story "The Third and Final Continent" eats cornflakes for breakfast, lunch, and dinner while he waits for his wife to join him from Calcutta. Or the wealthy Pranab Kaku, in "Hell–Heaven" from *Unaccustomed Earth*, who had never so much as poured himself a glass of water back home. ("Life as a graduate student in Boston was a cruel shock, and in his first month he lost nearly twenty pounds.")

Who are these men who cannot feed themselves without a wife? Who are these men who need to be reminded to take baths? Is the smell of their own sweat not a sufficient alarm—*now, it's bath time*? If men are so powerful, as efficient and intelligent as they claim to be, surely they can pick up dirty clothes from the floor and deposit them in the washing machine?

"Do Indian men know how to use washing machines?" I write down in a notebook, as I contemplate my cat. Have they entered kitchens even once in their lives? Do they know where anything is kept?

"Arré, date a *firangi*," says my friend, when I bring up the subject. "At least they know how to cook a basic meal and they help out around the house. Do you want a husband or a baby?"

I am struck by the acute truth of this. I am not maternal—I have never been a maternal person. The thought of a needy husband horrifies me. I'd have to pick up his shirts. I'd have to wash his dirty underwear. I'd have to be there when he complained about his boss, about the late nights at office (at least he would get to *clock out* of his job. Mine would be full time).

Besides, there was something profoundly unsexy about the notion of a helpless man. I was pretty sure James Bond knew how to sear his rib-eye or how to make the bed after he got done rumpling it with one of his villainesses. He knew how to build his own life from the ground up—a full, satisfying, adult life. All on his own. Would the Indian men I knew be able to do the same?

"You know what? I don't think I want a husband or a baby!"

Who can find a virtuous woman? For her price is far above rubies.

The heart of her husband doth safely trust in her, so that he shall have no need of spoil.

She will do him good and not evil all the days of her life.

She seeketh wool, and flax, and worketh willingly with her hands.

She is like the merchants' ships; she bringeth her food from afar.

She riseth also while it is yet night, and giveth meat to her household, and a portion to her maidens.

She considereth a field, and buyeth it: with the fruit of her hands she planteth a vineyard.

She girdeth her loins with strength, and strengtheneth her arms.

She perceiveth that her merchandise is good: her candle goeth not out by night.

She layeth her hands to the spindle, and her hands hold the distaff.

She stretcheth out her hand to the poor; yea, she reacheth forth her hands to the needy.

She is not afraid of the snow for her household: for all her household are clothed with scarlet.

She maketh herself coverings of tapestry; her clothing is silk and purple.

Her husband is known in the gates, when he sitteth among the elders of the land.

She maketh fine linen, and selleth it; and delivereth girdles unto the merchant.

Strength and honor are her clothing; and she shall rejoice in time to come.

She openeth her mouth with wisdom; and in her tongue is the law of kindness.

She looketh well to the ways of her household, and eateth not the bread of idleness.[5]

We spend so much time categorizing women, looking them over. Assessing them. Counting their virtues. They must do *this*, and be *that*, and have *these*, and bring *those*. Women are shown the mold from the beginning—"this is what you must fit into"—while men are not aware of the mold at all. There is no mold for a lovable man. For a marriageable man. Other than the ability to earn money.

I think of what happened when Tinder came to India. Indian men swarmed online forums, Reddit, Yahoo! Answers. They were convinced that something must have gone wrong with their app because they were being left-swiped. For the first time, they experienced rejection, and it was a stunning idea to them—the idea that they could be evaluated as easily as they evaluated women (and dismissed as easily). Men who had done no personality work whatsoever, men who had never devoted a single second to worrying about their presentation, or their looks, or their conversation, were being rejected *en masse*. And it horrified them.

There was something painfully satisfying in that story. For a tiny moment, a fraction of justice was restored.

Here's the thing. I'm twenty-nine years old, which is, oh, fifty-nine in *desi* years. My grandmother started saying a long time ago that her only wish is to see me get married. (As the only surviving grandparent, this statement has the rhetorical power of an M16 assault rifle.) Full disclosure: my aunt and uncle have made me a profile on Bharat Matrimony. I had never even *heard* of Bharat Matrimony.

Of course, I've thought about it. I know that, technically, there are benefits of getting married. Legal benefits. Financial benefits. (A two-income household would really come in handy for a struggling artist!) Society would smile approvingly at me and I'd always have a date to anything I wanted to go to. I'd never need to worry about getting a ride home or my physical safety in dodgy areas. A *man* would always be there—in all his glorious *manhood*—to protect me. Best of all, I'd never have to download Tinder ever again. *Hmm.*

I told my parents that I was open to the idea of getting an arranged marriage. Knowing me as they do, they were instantly (and rightly) suspicious.

Papa: Should I start looking for a boy?

Me: Sure! Here's a list of things I require.

My father was already starting to look nervous, but I began ticking off my fingers:

1) Financially solvent
2) Reasonably good-looking (There's some wiggle room here, but I refuse to compromise entirely. Not as long as paunchy thirty-year-olds with fast-receding hairlines felt entitled to

women who looked like they could be in Bollywood item numbers.)
3) Reasonably intelligent
4) Kind
5) No substance abuse issues
6) Supportive friends (so I didn't have to be his therapist)
7) A good temper
8) An open mind, free of any kind of bigotry or stubbornness[6]

There was a brief silence in which I could feel them weighing my demands.

Papa: Well, that's not so bad. That's not much to ask for.

Me, *shaking head sadly*: You don't know what it's *like*. You guys got married at twenty-five. You're as innocent as babes in the wood. But by all means, send any boys you find to Delhi. I'm happy to meet them.

And thus we come to the apex, to the zenith, to the *prestige*, to the fucking curtain call, to the moment we have all been waiting for, ladies and gentlemen, roll right up for the performance of a lifetime, the *bride-seeing*. This is it, the opportunity to showcase how ... *homely* you are, how crisp your samosas, how peppery your pudina chutney. Even if you're not inviting the would-be groom to your house to taste your wares, you are expected to be demure and womanly, eyes on the ground, presented for inspection.

Unless you're me.

Priya's Ten-step Technique for Putting off Desi Suitors

1) Show up slightly drunk
2) Show up in something distinctly un-sanskaari, like the much-reviled "spaghetti"
3) Order food before he does. Ask him patronizingly what he wants
4) Order more drinks
5) Talk about your sex life
6) Ask him about his sex life (Bonus option for the truly shameless: ask him about his sexual performance)
7) Declare that you are "child free"
8) Interrupt him frequently
9) Say "no" frequently
10) The killer—ask him how much money he makes and sound unimpressed by the answer

---

Jokes aside.

What I can tell you, except what we all already know, is that being a desi woman is about performance. Desi women are expected to be quiet, still, watchful, beautiful, and serene (no matter what complicated emotions may arise in us). As untroubled and secluded as a lotus in a walled courtyard. We are meant to create an atmosphere of simplicity, warmth, and comfort. Eternally, we are air hostesses, welcoming you into a strange place. We are homemakers. We make homes. We are homely. And we are constantly being evaluated, being rated and measured for how well we can perform homeliness.

This is what I'm rejecting. I am not simple, I'm not homely. I don't like to cook. I'm sulky and childish by turns, not always maternal. I expect my husband to be just as diligent and virtuous as the men in the Bible, as committed to making a safe and peaceful home for us. I don't ask the world of him, I only want him to bring as much to the marriage as I do. When I come home tired from work, I need him to comfort me as much as I do him.

I don't want to be trapped at home while my husband goes out. I don't want my world to be confined to the kitchen, the nursery, and the bedroom. I don't want my conversation to be restricted to what the maid did today. My horizons are large, broad, as sweeping as any man's and I will go out and explore them.

I don't want to stand in the corner of a room, holding a heavy tray, while my husband beckons me with one finger, as if I were a dog. I don't want to stand at the dinner table, my face burning in humiliation, as a man rejects the chapatis I have labored over. *I don't want to.* Let those words come out of my mouth, for once. Finally. I am not a "homely" girl. I think I can live with that.

Why I'm No Longer Talking to White People about Arranged Marriage

I have to be honest about something—if I were white, I would probably ask my Indian friends a lot of creepy questions about arranged marriage. I'm sorry.

Arranged marriage is a wildly complex way of bringing together two people. Anybody who says they aren't interested in hearing about it is lying through their teeth. I *know* white Americans are interested. (I know this because of the number of people who have asked me about it over the years. Usually at completely inappropriate times, like at my law school graduation. "I'm just saying, it's so heartwarming that you didn't succumb to the pressure of getting an arranged marriage!")

The thing about arranged marriage is that it's not exclusive to us. It's as old as the concept of soap. (It's marriage for love that's the shocking new concept.) Arranged marriage is *right there* on the very first page of *Pride and Prejudice*, which means that no English major anywhere in the world has an excuse for ignorance:

"Is he married or single?"

"Oh, single, my dear, to be sure! A single man of large fortune; four or five thousand a year. What a fine thing for our girls!"

"How so? How can it affect them?"

"My dear Mr. Bennet," replied his wife, "how can you be so tiresome! You must know that I am thinking of his marrying one of them."

The rest of the book bangs on about the great love between Elizabeth and Mr. Darcy, but this is the crucial passage. This book is a story about arranged marriages.

Love Marriages in *P&P*:

1) Elizabeth and Mr. Darcy (NB: she says her attraction was based in part on his huge mansion)
2) Jane and Mr. Bingley

Arranged Marriages in *P&P*:

1) Charlotte and Mr. Collins
2) Lydia and Mr. Wickham
3) Anne de Bourgh and Mr. Darcy (if she hadn't been "sickly," which is probably code for TB)
4) The other sisters
5) Caroline Bingley (probably)
6) Mrs. Bennet

Mrs. Bennet is the quintessential Indian *aunty* at a wedding—she maneuvers every social situation such that two compatible people can meet. She might sound like a human dating app (Indians living abroad often compare arranged marriage to Match.com) but in truth, she is far more efficient than any dating app. Dating apps only show you what a person would *like* to be seen as. Even a first date isn't a real date—it's somebody who's sent their lawyer to make a good case for them.

One of the most pressing concerns of white people is how impersonal arranged marriage is. "How can you get married to a person without knowing anything about them?" they cry, as if marriage wasn't, by definition, a bizarre contract. You might know your spouse's favorite color or their preferred brand of toothpaste, but there are so many ways in which human beings are unknowable. Every day—every *single* day—there's a story in the papers about a wife of fourteen years discovering her husband's hidden *sex slave in the attic*. At this point, I think we have to admit that we, as a species, are beautifully trusting and fatally stupid. We can absolutely get married to a person without knowing anything about them. We can stay married to a person for fourteen years and take their word for it that the bizarre noises from the attic are merely the wind knocking over a bucket full of mops.

Arranged marriage can't solve this problem entirely, of course. But it goes a long way towards it.

There is an old fairy tale—bloody in the way that all fairy tales were before Disney bowdlerized them—called "Mr. Fox." In it, a mysterious young man woos and wins over a beautiful woman. Before they get married, she sneaks off to investigate his castle and discovers his horrible secret: he's a Bluebeard type who kills all his wives.

That is exactly the kind of story for which an aunty exists to prevent. In a brown context, there is no chance that our Mr. Fox would have remained mysterious. From the day he rode up to woo his lady, the aunties of the family would have made extensive inquiries into his antecedents. ("Mary, it turns out that Mr. Fox has been married thirty times before and all his neighbors say that Castle Fox smells of blood. The marriage is off.")

When my cousin was looking for a bride, I remember going through some girls' profiles. The first thing that struck me was how incredibly detailed they were. They included the girl's family tree, a complete medical history, a family medical history, financial statements, educational background, and every CV she had ever had. Incredibly, they even included the fact that she had been on the basketball team in high school. (I tried to think of a way in which this could be classified as necessary information. I failed.)

It was clear that nothing would be allowed to slip through the cracks.

* * *

The other inevitable question that white people have on arranged marriages: "Are *you* going to get one?"

I never know how to respond to this question. To me, it's the same as asking whether I'll get a tattoo. If I'm bored, maybe. I make it a habit not to take a definitive stance on things like that. I don't want to say "No, I'll NEVER EVER in my life EVER get a tattoo." Then I'd look really stupid when I got one.[1]

There are two Priyas warring in my head. Good Priya wants to be polite. Bad Priya wants to flip the script.

Bad Priya, *in a leather jacket, smoking Marlboro Reds*: Well, do you think you'll go the other route and marry some dude you met at the bar six months ago? Whose mother you haven't even met? One of those what-d'you-call-'ems—weird love marriages that are based entirely on fleeting sexual desire and are therefore bound to fail?

Unfortunately, Good Priya always wins, so I answer with: "Well, I don't know." This answer, I have learned, is the wrong answer to give. White people are never satisfied with this answer. I can feel it on their lips, the struggle to not say, "*But whyyyyyyyyyyyyyyyyy?*"

It's the wrong question to ask. Who, if they had the chance to meet a decent, financially solvent, reasonably attractive, and intelligent man from a good family background, would decline? It's no more labor than a Tinder date and potentially much more rewarding. (The average Tinder date is waxing your legs in order to split a meal you can't afford with a man you have to let down gently at the end of the night.)

I tell them: "You know I can say no, right? It's very simple . . . my parents introduce me to a man and we have a cup of coffee or get dinner together. And if I don't like him, or he doesn't like me, we can say 'no.' It's not as if every meeting leads to marriage. You generally meet quite a few people before you find the one you're compatible with. Just like in real life."

They don't know what to do with that information. They stir their coffee while they try to think of another objection.

I wonder how many of them watch *The Bachelor*.

The Bachelor is a deeply grotesque television show that has somehow become part of the very fabric of American culture. The essential premise is this: twenty-five women (or men, if it's *The Bachelorette*) gather in a house to compete for the affections of an absolute stranger. Meanwhile, the bachelor has two months to select a fiancée from the women present. During this process, the contestants are not allowed TV or cell phones; they are completely cut off from the world outside the Bachelor mansion. They spend their time fixing their hair, arguing, and waiting around for the bachelor to give them plastic roses.

Throughout the season, the contestants and the bachelor give interviews in which they repeatedly say, "This is a dream come true." *It's an absolute fairy tale*, chirps Kimberly, twenty-four, as she adjusts her too-tight diamanté gown. *I'm the luckiest girl in the world!*[2]

I wonder how people can watch *The Bachelor* without seeing that it's the less-honest version of an arranged marriage.

* * *

It's not the questions I resent, it's the tone. It's the "why is your culture so WEIRD?" tone. Americans' entire knowledge of "the weirdness of Indian culture" has been gleaned from watching Bollywood movie trailers of the 1990s.

Facts about American Culture Entirely Based on Watching American TV Shows

1) People are super fashionable during the winters and in the summers they wear bikinis.
2) Everybody has a boyfriend. Boyfriends are more important than homework.
3) You can drink tap water directly without dying from typhoid.
4) Jam is called jelly, but jam is also called jam.
5) Teenagers get an incredible amount of stuff done in the hours between waking up and going to school.
6) When Americans are going through something difficult, they take a long walk or sit on a cold park bench at sunset to do something called "clearing their minds."
7) It's fine to call your mom a bitch if you really want to.
8) There's no difference between inside clothes and outside clothes.
9) Breakfast is seven waffles, ten pancakes, three glasses of orange juice, five pieces of bacon, and two plates of eggs. You leave 99.4 percent of it on the plate.
10) When shop assistants ask if you need help, you say "no, I'm good" regardless of whether you are, in fact, good.

To me, American culture was the strangest of all, with its seductive focus on the individual instead of the community. Nowhere is this more apparent than at American weddings. A while ago, I read one of those "Dear Polly" columns. It was from a distressed woman who wanted to know if she could revoke her sister's plus-one for her (the distressed's) wedding.

I can't remember precisely, but the gist was

Dear Polly,

My sister has always been the pretty one in the family. She's recently acquired a stunning boyfriend. If she brings him to my wedding, all the attention will be on them!!! Polly!!!!!! I don't want all the attention to be on them! It's MY wedding. Please tell me it's reasonable to ask her to come alone.

Yours,
I hate my sister xx

If you Google "upstaged at my wedding," you'll find hundreds of thousands of similar cries of anguish. They range from the reasonable—*I'm upset because somebody else proposed at my wedding!*—to the downright sociopathic—*how can I make sure nobody in my bridal party is pretty?*[23]

I don't think the women who ask these questions are horrible people. I don't think the "Dear Polly" letter is from a woman who actually hates her sister. What I do think is that we set these women up for failure when we tell them, "This is *your day* and you deserve a perfect wedding!"

This is what we're told about Perfect™ weddings:

1) Weddings are the most important and romantic day of our lives and everyone is obligated to pay full attention to us during every second of that day.

2) Our bridesmaids must look elegant but not upstage us. They are baby rosebuds arranged around us, the queen rose. Therefore, they must purchase and wear dresses in matching shades of eggplant.

3) The ceremony should bring a tear to the eye of the most cynical bachelor.

I respectfully submit that this is an extremely high-pressure list of demands. This list is the reason why brides have nervous breakdowns the night before their weddings, thinking of all the things that could go wrong.[4]

This list is the reason they turn into bridezillas and a cold war breaks out between them and the maid of honor (a phenomenon that has been thoroughly documented by Hollywood movies). I thought of the dreaded WhatsApp chat that so many of my friends had complained about: the one that resulted in your phone blowing up with a billion notifications (at all hours) about the most banal updates. If you've ever attended a north Indian wedding, you know that it is an entirely different animal.

For one thing, brown people aren't content with one measly ceremony. The average Indian wedding stretches over three days, which should satisfy the most attention-hungry bride.[5]

It also means that she's less likely to Google "wedding ruined by bitch sister."

Equally important: it is very difficult to upstage a north Indian Hindu bride. This is partly due to the fact that she wears six yards of flaming red silk and enough gold to drown a kitten. But unlike in south Indian weddings, you're encouraged to *try*.

Suggested dress code: Don't even think of showing up in something casual or restrained. Think "rapper's birthday party" when you're choosing outfits! The bride will love it!!!

When I was getting ready for my first north Indian wedding, I asked my mother what I should wear. She said, "Oh, I've laid out something on your bed."

I ran back to my room to look at it. My first thought was *help!* because it was a purple salwar-kameez tunic with green and golden pants and a matching golden scarf. It weighed about seven pounds and was impressively neon.

"*MAAAAAAAAaaaaaaaaAAAAAAAAAAAAAAAAAAAAAAAaa aaaaaaaaaaaaaa!*" I bellowed in anguish.

"IT'S EITHER THIS OR THE PINK-AND-GOLD BUSTIER LEHENGA!" she shouted back with the ease of someone who had mastered the art of emotional blackmail.

Forty minutes later, we were pulling up in front of the wedding venue—a farmhouse in one of Delhi's posher neighborhoods. It was lit up like the set of a particularly lurid Baz Luhrmann movie. A pool glittered darkly in the background.

"Aren't we late?" I said.

"No, it's only 10:30 p.m. North Indian weddings don't really get going until midnight."

To my relief, my mother had been right about the clothes. Everybody appeared to be dipped in neon pink and blue and gold. The only color that was nowhere to be seen was white (the traditional color of mourning in Hinduism). I was—by far—the most restrained person there.

For the first twenty minutes, I didn't do much beside walking around open-mouthed. There was a wedding rapper *and* a wedding DJ. There was one tent full of flowers and another tent just for desserts. Every single tree on the premises had been covered with fairy lights, Chinese lanterns, and strings of white jasmine that smelled like cheap perfume. The wedding planner had run mad.

It was flamboyance on a scale I'd never seen before. But, somehow, none of that was as impressive as the fact that *everybody was also having fun.* To my left, aunties were sizing up eligible marriage prospects for their daughters ("He is 5'11", settled in the US . . . computer engineering") and appraising the cost of everything with an expert eye.

"Two lakhs for the flowers itself."

"No, no, what are you saying, Reema? One lakh only. How are the kebabs?"

"So-so," sighed aunty #1, eating mutton kebabs faster than I could count. "Must have been very expensive. Should have got the catering done from a cheaper place."

I turned away to hide a smile. This, I realized, was the biggest compliment they could think of.

On my right, young men were getting roaring drunk on imported whiskey. Tiny children staggered in and out of the dessert tent, their faces dunked in powdered sugar.

When I finally caught a glimpse of the bride, I saw her in a whirl of silks, dancing to the latest Punjabi song. She was beautiful as every bride is on her wedding day, but more importantly, she was the merriest bride I'd ever seen. A group of young women surrounded her, their lehengas swishing like giant bells on the dance floor. The groom wasn't even dancing.[6]

I thought back to the handful of Western weddings I'd attended, where the photographer took dewy photos of couples clasping each other while the band sang Fleetwood Mac covers. I marveled at how different this wedding was: how . . . unsentimental. Nobody was crying, not even the baby who was now sick of sweets. Even if a drunken uncle made a ribald joke, nobody would care.[7] It was a wedding that had embraced chaos. Much like my people. I got a plate of lamb biryani, sat at a table meant for somebody else, and watched the dancing, reveling in every bit of my weird and wonderful culture.

VIII
INDEPENDENCE

The Story of an Air Conditioner

Like everybody from a solidly upper-middle-class background in India, I grew up with a maid.

It's kind of a strange thing to have a maid. No, not kind of. It's absolutely *mad*. The very notion of a maid is mad when you consider that she is somebody who will pick up your dirty clothes because you're too lazy to pick them up yourself. A maid washes your dirty underwear. A maid wipes your filthy plates, scrubs your toilets, buffs the floor of your bathrooms, and cuts you another slice of fresh toast with butter. The idea of a human being whose job is to cater to you 24-7 is appalling. Or it should be, in a civilized society.[1] Wash your goddamn dirty underwear yourself, you jackal!

When you grow up in India, you lose sight of normalcy. Especially if you're a boy. It becomes protocol for you to leave your dirty clothes on your bed, to get up from the dining table without pushing your chair back in, to rely on your maid gently waking you up in the morning instead of setting an alarm. Somebody else will take care of it. No problem, bro.

On the scale of spoiled, I would say I was about a 4/5. I was certainly not as spoiled as a rich industrialist's son or a Bollywood star kid. I was raised to study hard, to spend my evenings at my homework table instead of the cricket field or in front of the TV. And yet, I was spoiled. I had a maid and anybody who has had a maid has been spoiled rotten.

I didn't quite realize how spoiled I was until I went to America. America is a wonderful place that way because *nobody cares* who you are. Not a single, solitary person knows or cares that you're Mr. Luthra's son or that you're an IAS daughter. In America—unless you're legitimately a millionaire—you'll still have to wash your dishes yourself, do your own grocery shopping, pick up your dirty underwear.

Mop the floor.

During my first year in college, I took up a part-time job in Food Services to earn extra money per week (the college fees were burning a hole in my parents' bank account and it felt awful to ask them for anything for myself). I didn't exactly know what Food Services meant (drizzling raspberry coulis on a slice of cheesecake?) but I was convinced it couldn't be hard.

The first day on the job, they handed me a mop and a foamy bucket. "Go on, scrub the kitchen floor."

Scrub? Like Cinderella? I looked at the bucket, then at the mop, then at the tired face of my supervisor. I deduced that I was supposed to dunk the mop *in* the bucket and then somehow wash the dingy floor with the wet mop. One quick (Christian) prayer later, I began scrubbing.

Three minutes later, they were all staring at me.

It was an uncomfortable kind of stare. It was the kind of stare you might reserve for a puppy with, say, green markings. You aren't screaming about it—it's not, like, a *headless* puppy—but you're watching the puppy go about its business, completely absorbed by the unusual sight. Green markings? Why? How?

I sneaked a quick look at my mop. Was I holding it the wrong way? Was I swabbing the floor in an incorrect direction? I reversed the motion, and they went from surprised to aghast.

"Here," said one of the line cooks, stepping forward and taking it from me. He spoke quietly as if he were mentioning something deeply distressing. "I'll show you how to do it."

He placed my fingers over the mop. "That's how you hold it. And *that's* how you should scrub the floor with it. Oh, and you don't need so much water. You're creating a . . . sea, the way you're doing it."

I mopped the floor the way he taught me for some minutes, in complete silence. It was only broken by one of the other girls, an international student from a country where they clearly didn't have maids.

"How come you don't know how to use a mop?" she said in her high, fluty voice. "Are you an Indian princess?"

I wish I could say it were only the chores that were unfamiliar. I had never really thought about it but I saw now how insulated I had been in India. You see, in India, you barely interact with strangers. If you're a young girl, you're certainly not encouraged to go out on your own and talk to people you don't know. On the few occasions you meet strangers—say some of your parents' colleagues are coming to dinner—you are introduced to them by your parents.

"Come out, Leela, don't be shy. This is that nice uncle you met last time, remember? Say hi to him and his wife. They've come all the way from Calicut just to meet you!"

At this point, I would trace frantic arabesques in the carpet with my toes. In agonies of shyness, I refused to raise my eyes to theirs. I resented my parents for wanting to parade their children as if we were piano-playing seals. "Why don't you show the nice aunty how well you can recite/draw/play the veena/do karate kicks/elocute/repeat the multiplication table!"

But even in those most uncomfortable moments, there were always people who acted as buffers between me and the world. If I needed to go buy toothpaste or sanitary napkins, a driver and maid would accompany me to the store (on the rare occasions that I needed to go to the store at all). This may seem like a tremendous luxury—and indeed it is, but it also left me feeling like Princess Jasmine. If I couldn't do anything alone, how was I supposed to feel like I *could* do anything at all?

And yet, Indian women are incredibly capable. (Some are more. The women in Delhi have hard faces and aren't afraid to bargain with a shopkeeper until he's on his knees.) However, the chrysalis-transformation that this necessitates is a mystery to me, when you consider the imperatives to be modest and shrinking and completely dependent on others. It's a terrible coyness in the culture, one that encourages us to be dainty violets instead of the big, strong trees that we actually are. For every Shubha Mudgal who sings in her naturally powerful, husky voice, we have a million unbearably sweet Shreya Ghoshal–wannabes, who quaver and lilt their way through dainty soprano solos.[2] So soft that you can barely make the words out. *Modesty is all.*

Take engagement pictures. Ye gods, engagement pictures.

I had never considered the problem with Indian engagement pictures until I saw my ex's. When they surfaced on Facebook, I immediately began clicking through each photo in an obsessive ritual that is familiar to all exes the world over.

These pictures, I noted, were markedly different from American engagement photos. The white couples I'd seen get engaged were photographed holding hands, smiling at each other. Some of them were a little kitschier: they were riding horses or sipping wine on an improbably green-looking knot of grass. But in almost all the photos, they had *normal* expressions. Like they'd known each other at least five minutes before the photographer bawled: "GOUDA!"

My ex, in sharp contrast, looked like he had never met his bride-to-be. What were the instructions for *this* shoot?

"Sir, now remember you are a villain from a Dharmendra film. Twist your moustache, as if you have one. Now grab Madam's hand. Madam look away, *look away*, LOOK AWAY; act coy. Remember, you've never seen a man before. You are seeing a man today for the FURST time. It is scaring you! You are very scared and shy. Sir, you are chasing ma'am. You are chasing her and you are catching her and you are tying her to the railway tracks if she is not falling for your seduction. Now, let's try another pose—from behind. Sir, you are catching ma'am FROM BEHIND and holding her stomach. Stand stiffly, sir. More stiffly. Ma'am, don't forget to look down. Don't look at sir. I-want-to-escape feel *aa gayi*."

I haven't given much thought to how I want my engagement photos to look, but I am quite certain that I don't want them to scream *help me*.

Of course, this valorization of helpless women isn't limited to desis. I boggled the first time I heard the American expression: "How can I help you, little lady?" Online, I am well acquainted with men's urges to help women. Their inexplicably powerful boner to teach women how to do things, to educate women, and to offer terrible or blindly obvious solutions to our problems. It is, I muse, quite the aphrodisiac. If you wanted to make a man fall in love with you, what better way than to ask him to teach you tennis? As Margaret Atwood wrote in her poem "Siren Song":

> [. . .] This song
> is a cry for help: Help me!
> Only you, only you can,
> you are unique
> at last. Alas
> it is a boring song
> but it works every time.

But I would argue, all things considered, that us Indians have a particular fetish for damsels in distress. Helpless, flinching, wincing, painfully coy women. The "good woman" in the Bollywood film, you'll find, is generally fairly incompetent. It's the vixen who is the bad bitch, who's accomplished enough to mastermind the plot and smoke a villainous-looking cigarette while ruining good men's lives.

My friend Apurva says that this is excellent, that we can use this to our advantage. "Priya, have you ever gone to an office to get some bureaucratic red tape handled? The men are hopeless. The only way to get anything done is to come in with your dupatta over your head and to smile shyly at them, fold your hands, and say, '*Namaste Uncleji. I'm so lost, can you help me?*'"

For those first precarious years in America, I didn't need to fake helplessness. I stumbled through the world like Gretel without a trail of crumbs to follow. At least when I was in college, I had certain things I could take for granted—like dorms, reliable plumbing, meal plans. I didn't need to charm strangers or get my phone line installed efficiently. Every single thing I did on my own—including opening a simple checking account—felt like a Himalayan task.

"I hadn't expected America to be so *difficult*," I sighed to my mother on Skype. I'd just moved into a new apartment (thereby incurring serious lumbar injuries; it didn't have an elevator and I'd had to carry boxes up four flights all day). "There's just no one around, you know? No relatives or boyfriend."

My parents wanted to know why I couldn't ask a neighbor.

"Um, no," I said, thinking of how it would be back home. Where we knew our neighbors and could drop in unannounced. "You can't ask people for help here."

I'd said it casually but it seemed to me to reveal a dark truth about the heart of America: that although people were very nice (asking you about your day and smiling when they handed you your latte), *they expected you to do things on your own.*

A friend confirmed this suspicion when she told me a story of moving into an American dorm in college.

"I'd got along very well with my suitemates: we'd go out dancing, get food, and talked. But one day, in the middle of the night, I woke up with a terrible allergic rash. I didn't know what was happening to me and I felt horrible, so I did the only thing I could think of to do: I rapped on a suitemate's door. When she opened, I tearfully told her that I wasn't well. I guess I expected her to react like somebody would have back home, you know. Or like I would have: if that had been me, I would have taken her to a doctor right away. But not this girl, she couldn't be bothered . . . She stared at my face, said briskly, 'Yeah, you'll want to go to the Health Center about that,' and shut the door in my face. Not meanly. Just, you know, she wouldn't help."

"It's an individualist society," I said. "Like, everybody lives in their own houses and it's all so sequestered . . . people don't live as a community, do they?"

I thought of the wide open spaces that I had traveled across in America and how many more of them there were. Texas, the South, the mountains, and the dusty rose of the Utah desert . . . America seemed vast, with so few people to occupy all that land. Of course, they had to get used to doing things on their own.

There was a beauty in it, I thought. Self-sufficiency is always attractive. Maybe not when you're old or ill. That's when you long for community. But when you're healthy and young, why not live by yourself? Why not learn to do things by yourself?

I was constantly in awe of the things my American friends knew how to do: their taxes, driving stick, gourmet cooking, Ikea furniture installation, erecting tents when they went camping, basic plumbing, even how to treat wounds (nobody wanted to pay hospital bills). So many of them had worked service jobs as teenagers and they knew how to make a caramel macchiato in the sexiest possible way.[3] In contrast, I often felt like a bumbler, shy and ineffectual.

That ended with an air conditioner.

It was, I remember, one of the most brutal summers of my life. I'd just accepted a summer internship at the Middlesex DA's office and they'd asked if I had a car.

"No," I said, but promised them I could use public transport. (In a long list of Bad Priya decisions, this would turn out to rank spectacularly high.)

When I looked it up, I figured out that I'd have to walk to the nearest subway station, hop on the Green Line, switch subway trains at Back Bay to the Orange Line, and travel for an hour *before* a twenty-five-minute walk to the DA's office. I told myself that this would be easy, that I could do it five days a week for three months with minimal discomfort. As long as I got up a little earlier each day.

It was the second warmest summer on record.

I'm no stranger to hot weather—I'm *Indian*—but that summer beggars description. It was so hot that people fainted in subways. Nobody went outside: everyone stayed in their air-conditioner-cooled houses and called taxis to the movie theaters. It was so hot outside that I looked longingly at the beautiful, quietly gleaming Charles River and seriously contemplated jumping off the bridge into it. There was barely any point showering (which I did first thing in the mornings): five minutes into my walk to the station, I was invariably sweating through my light top. By the end of the journey, I had to put on my suit jacket just to cover the armpit-sweat stains.

Somehow, staying in was even worse. My apartment (like most typical Boston apartments) had no ceiling fan. These were old apartment buildings that were only equipped for the cold. What could I do? I opened my windows, bought huge packs of ice, and laid wet clothes all over the apartment because Google told me that this would "cool down the atmosphere considerably." I slept completely naked. And still, *still*, I stewed and had nightmares about ovens and ship furnaces.

The day I read that it would hit 100 degrees, I decided to buy an air conditioner.

I couldn't afford an expensive air conditioner (I was so broke I bought $0.99 tins of Goya chickpeas and ate them with hot sauce for most meals), but I *could* afford a used one. I'd have nobody to drop off or install my AC. I'd have to do it myself. The taxi ride from the store would cost too much.

I decided to take the subway.

After parting reluctantly with a wad of cash, I was now the proud owner of a brand new secondhand air conditioner.

"You okay to carry that out on your own?" said the cashier laconically. He looked about nineteen and no more muscular than me.

"YES," I said indignantly. "Absolutely."

Six steps later, I realized that I was not, in fact, fine. In fact, I was staggering under the weight of the box.

Maybe if I had worked out regularly, lifted weights, had a hint of musculature, I could have carried this breezily out the door. I could have one arm on the AC, winking nonchalantly at strangers. Look at me! I can carry this huge box easily!

Instead, I was gasping. It felt like all the nerves in my arm were being pinched with pliers. I didn't even know I *had* so many nerves. Was everybody just walking around with all these nerves inside them? It seemed excessive.

Little by little, I made my way home. I had to stop to set it down at various intervals: on people's stoops, on a seat on the subway (a pregnant woman looked at me in indignation, but I felt sure I was carrying more than her), and then out on the street again, just when I felt my back couldn't take it any more.

A homeless man snickered at me when I set it down near him. "Lady, you need a boyfriend to be carrying all that for you."

I sighed. This would never be a problem at home, I thought. At home—by which I mean India—I'd never have to worry about stuff like this. Anybody who moved house, for instance, had a host of people to help them do things. No middle-class woman would be carrying heavy boxes alone. She probably would be shamed if she did. ("Why is Anjali Mehta carrying that? Doesn't she have *servants?*")

Sweating, dying, cramping, and struggling, I inched my way down the last street. There it was, my apartment building, rising high and glorious above me. I'd still have to get it up the steps, but I figured that could wait. I sat down next to my box and stretched my poor legs out.

It was sunset, and I plugged in my iPod. The high, sweet voice of Katy Perry—2012's biggest new artist—came on and I watched everybody walk past me. I closed my eyes, letting the last of the sun bake my eyelids. Nobody on the pavement knew what I'd done—carried an AC home myself, which I was going to install later. They didn't know. But I knew, and that was enough.

Closing Prayer: For My Strong Brown Women

"Woman and the earth have to tolerate a lot."

—Meena Kumari, *Kaajal*

I want you to know that I see you there, girl walking home from school with your braids crossed over. I see how you walk a little more slowly than the others, how you catch your dupatta when it falls down. You do not swagger like a boy but shuffle. When you wear skirts, you sit so carefully that nobody can glimpse your coltish legs. You learned these manners young. There is nothing carefree about you. I see that your eyes are downcast and that you clutch your schoolbook as though it were precious stuff. Your eye and cheek are subdued; not filled with the natural radiance and carelessness of youth. It is the sobriety of someone who has learned discipline too early; it is the back that has known—too often—a heavy hand. It has known all kinds of burdens, your young back. It has known the cane of the schoolteacher, ah yes, but above these, it has learned the blows of a thousand commonplace indignities at home. Your shoulders are not squared but hesitant;

you have not had occasion to learn that you ought to be proud. You are still learning which adjectives are the good ones and which contradictions to hold like a fix'd star in your body: you are a woman early. Far, far too early.

I see you, too, housewife caught in the middle of her day. Bargaining at the *sabzi mandi*, wiping your hand across your forehead because you got too little sleep last night and you were awake early this morning to make your children's tiffin (neat sandwiches with the crusts cut off; that was what your children learned from TV, they learned to want sandwiches cut the American way). I see the half-hearted kohl that is your only concession to makeup. I see your cotton sari limp and flagging in the heat of the city at 3 P.M. You are not thin after the second child, not like those women you sometimes steal glimpses of (when the kids aren't watching their shows, when the husband isn't watching his matches) on TV. Your body is not aerobicized nor dieted to perfection. You eat what everybody else eats (and after they eat). There is so little in your day to look forward to. Perhaps, this is what accounts for the weariness in your voice now, as you order another kilo of lauki, and the vegetable man ties it up with good rough twine. You must go home now and you must look after your husband's mother: poor wandering woman with Alzheimer's. I see how this is the only moment—the sole moment of privacy—in your day. (Even though it isn't, because there is always a man somewhere looking at a woman.) I see that you feel older than you are. So very old and tired early. Far, far too early.

I see you, working woman running to catch the metro. Struggling to find her place among the many surly men that throng the train each morning. There is something heartbreaking about the cheapness of your white shirts, your hair so carefully arranged into a ponytail that you hope it looks professional. These clothes are all you can afford because in this rich city you only have a monthly salary of 20,000 rupees and you have to send money back to your family in the village. It is for them that you are slaving: that is why you travel so far each morning and endure the familiarity of your boss when he leans over to comment on your work (you wince at the moments when he brushes your back). You joined the workforce early and you will stay there late—but not doing what you love, never doing what you love.

I see all of you and I ask: where do you go to cry? I have never seen you crying, not one of you. I have never seen you give way to those tears that surely must come thick and fast when you are trampled upon. I have not seen you squat down on your haunches in the middle of the day to cry out of sheer frustration because it feels, some days, like the weight of the world is on your narrow brown shoulders. When you hold your men close at night, when they sleep like children on your breasts to gather strength for their coming days, where do you turn? Where do you go to, to find solace when you cannot find it in his three fingers of Black Label? Is there a crying bathroom in your office, is there a special deserted corridor in the school that you go to in times of need? When the world is harsh with you (because it is, unrelentingly), where do you go to find your strength? Your children lean on you, but who do you lean on? Who will listen silently to your woes? Who cares? When you forgive others their transgressions (because forgiveness is demanded of you each time), who do you go to confess? When others take their frustration, their rage, and their grievances out on you, who do you take it out on? (Or do you eat it, refusing to pass on sorrow and pain as men do?) No therapists for you, no priests, no redeemers, nobody who will hold your feet in his lap when you come home worn out from your own private struggle with the world. No, for you there is nobody. Is it at night that you cry? Softly, so that your husband does not hear? My dear, there even the wall is thin, and you dare not let your shoulders shake or touch the unknowing man beside you. When have I seen even one of you be graceless or give way? Or scream aloud some of the rage inside you, the one that you have, too, just like men. Only you are not men and so you do not give way.

Sisters, dear ones, you are legion. When I think of the strength of Indian women, it is your faces I see. All your faces.

Notes

Shameless

1. The recitation of simple facts by women also qualify as bragging.
2. Anurag Verma, "How Desi Porn Search Terms Differ from the Rest of the World," HuffPost, 9 January 2017, https://www. huffingtonpost.in/2017/01/09/how-search-terms-for-porn-in-india-differ-from-rest-of-the-world_a_21650836/.
3. A person whose sense of gender corresponds to or matches their birth sex.

Men Who Masturbate

1. Masturbatory, https://en.wiktionary.org/wiki/masturbatory.
2. Masturbation appears an incredible number of times in C.K.'s oeuvre. He brings it up constantly and even tells a Christian woman on his show, who opposes it, "I'm going to masturbate later, and I'm going to think about you, and there's nothing you can do about it!" In retrospect, this is an incredibly cruel and offensive act. But when the revelations about C.K. were made, people said he couldn't have been capable of it—*completely ignoring* his well-documented obsession with masturbation.
3. "Louis C.K. Responds to Accusations: The Stories Are True," *New York Times*, 10 November 2017, https://www.nytimes. com/2017/11/10/arts/television/louis-ck-statement.html.

Uncomfortable Women

1. The trolley problem is a thought experiment in ethics. The general form of the problem is this:

    There is a runaway trolley barreling down the railway tracks. Ahead, on the tracks, there are five people tied up and unable to move. The trolley is headed straight for them.

    You are standing at some distance in the train yard, next to a lever. If you pull the lever, the trolley will switch to a different set of tracks. However, you notice that there is one person tied up on the sidetrack. You have two options:
    1) Do nothing, and the trolley kills the five people on the main track.
    2) Pull the lever, diverting the trolley on to the side track where it will kill one person.

    Which is the most ethical choice?
2. They held conferences and roundtables on: "Are Sweatshops as Bad as They Seem?" and "The Secret Benefits of Sweatshops." Cartoonishly racist and about as right-wing as you could get.
3. *Triggered* is also used to refer derisively to "snowflakes," sensitive people, or social justice warriors. "Oh, did I trigger you?" sneer men online, as if they gained some sort of moral victory over one instead of being hurtful.
4. I had always watched *Ally McBeal* and thought, "God, such fun, why can't I work in an office like that?" I had the privilege of not knowing what that meant. It meant lines being crossed. Constantly.
5. I told a male friend that it was late, that it was nearly dawn, and that I needed to go to bed. He set his glass down on the table—he had drunk enough for a whole table of people—and said he would call an Uber. I went up to my bedroom, where he followed me. He stood there, looking at me, as I got under the sheets. After another ten minutes, he left. I have no idea what he was thinking during those ten minutes. "What can I tell her? How can I convince her? What is the perfect combination of words that will make her give in?"

6. Katie Way, "I Went on a Date with Aziz Ansari. It Turned into the Worst Night of My Life," Babe, https://babe.net/2018/01/13/aziz-ansari-28355.
7. Interestingly, this is one of the very first Google results for Aziz Ansari.
8. Aziz Ansari, "Dick Pics," 7 October 2016, https://amara.org/en/videos/P96wMp2xOhfx/en/1400584/.

Beauty

1. *Arabian Nights* (Philadelphia, 1842), p. 393.
2. Jules Verne, *Around the World in Eighty Days* (1873), http://www.jules-verne.co.uk/around-the-world-in-80-days/ebook-page-29.asp.

Body

1. In that creepy way that we know celebrities' bodies better than our own.
2. Of course, that wasn't the case. I know that now. I'd bought copies of the *US Weekly* and *Star*, which talked about "Lindsay's New Bod!" and "Hilary Duff Buys Coke at Gas Station!"
3. Charlotte McDonald, "How Many Earths Do We Need?", BBC News, 16 June 2015, https://www.bbc.com/news/magazine-33133712.
4. In the updated rerelease of the books, the twins are size four.
5. Pro-anorexia.
6. Pro-bulimia.
7. I obsessively watched every single show where the protagonists were extremely thin women or girls. *90210. Desperate Housewives. The O.C.* And, of course, *Ally McBeal*, in which Calista Flockhart played a tiny woman with outsize emotions. I watched these shows as if I could absorb thinness through the screen.
8. Candia McWilliam, *A Little Stranger* (London: Bloomsbury, 2011).
9. Ibid., p. 116.

10. "Is This a Rupi Kaur Poem Or Some Shit We Made Up?" Babe, 8 March 2018, https://babe.net/2018/03/08/rupi-kaur-bad-poetry-40877.

11. Souradeep Roy, "Rupi Kaur's Bad Poems Shouldn't Worry Us—The Myopic View of the Literary Establishment Should," Scroll, 17 March 2018, https://scroll.in/article/872099/rupi-kaurs-bad-poems-shouldnt-worry-us-the-myopic-view-of-the-literary-establishment-should.

12. Paul Rohrbach, "Rupi Kaur's Poetry Needs Workshopping," *Cavalier Daily*, 18 October 2017, www.cavalierdaily.com/article/2017/10/rupi-kaurs-poetry-needs-workshopping.

13. Linsey Adler, "Instagram Poet Rupi Kaur Seems Utterly Uninterested in Reading Books," The Concourse, 10 April 2017, https://theconcourse.deadspin.com/instagram-poet-rupi-kaur-seems-utterly-uninterested-in-1819153164.

Dump Him

1. These are the kind of girls whose names remind you of Ikea tables. They are always very pretty but they have Ikea table names.
2. Source: Dating DJs.
3. Fruit of the Poisonous Tree Doctrine: you can't bring up evidence obtained illegally, because then the boyfriend can counter with "why were you snooping on my phone in the first place?"
4. Except alcoholics. They still need interventions.

Drama Ranis: Field Notes

1. The photo is old, but that's of no consequence: he just wants to prove to you that once upon a time, he met white people.
2. The most deadly weapon in the arsenal: the hypothetical question framed as an actual one.
3. Of course, this excessive ki-ki-ing and overreacting is for non-emergency situations. In *actual* emergency situations, brown mothers are competent, cool, and controlled. (Unlike brown

fathers, who sink into chairs and need to be revived with four pegs of Johnnie Walker Blue.)

4. When this actually happened in St. Thomas Central School—my alma mater—in 2017, the students were expelled. It was only when the incident made national headlines that the school board was willing to reconsider their punishment. A boy hugging his platonic friend (after she'd won a school prize) was apparently enough to destabilize the culture that they had worked so long to preserve. (Gopika Ajayan, "For a Hug and Photos, Kerala School Calls Teen a 'Bull in Heat', Expels Him: HC Agrees," News Minute, 15 December 2017, https://www.thenewsminute.com/article/hug-and-photos-kerala-school-calls-teen-bull-heat-expels-him-hc-agrees-73215.)

5. An Indian soap that ran over 2,000 episodes. Ostensibly a family saga about two sisters who strive to be perfect wives, but really about all sorts of things, including, but not limited to, demon babies, witches, sorceresses, people falling into comas, and many emotional slaps between family members.

6. A hypothesis: any culture that makes dramatic movies also produces dramatic people. My friend from college was Arab (we watched some deliciously dramatic movies together). In our freshman year, they put her on suicide watch for saying she wanted to die. She was amazed by this. I still remember her narrowing her heavily kohl-lined eyes at me and saying, "But, Priya, I didn't mean that I was actually going to kill myself?! I merely said that I wanted to die. Do Americans not say that they want to die sometimes?"

7. I felt that this, too, was a matter of time. I could easily picture myself changing my name to Pilar and moving to Bolivia to start over. If only for the reason that there were no nosy aunties in Bolivia. (As far as I know.)

8. My parents insisted on us hiking, an activity I despised. Why, I reasoned, would any sane person want to climb a mountain merely to climb back down? My parents would not listen and I hiked the path irately. Only to discover, *to my everlasting horror*, that there were leeches on both my legs. The long muddy grass was a perfect breeding ground for them, and by the time we reached the top I

had three on one leg and two on the other. Instead of informing anybody about my leech acquisition, I merely turned and stalked back down. I cannot explain why, but it felt like vindication to point to my pants later and say pathetically: "Look, I have leeches on my legs. I wanted to tell you. This is why hiking is bad." Dramatic people don't mind suffering as long as they can point it out later and say, "Look, how I suffered. What a martyr I was."

9. When I saw this maneuver executed in movies, I always laughed because surely no one in real life would bother to wait hours to confront their teen. Yes, it was a supremely dramatic gesture, but nobody was *that* dramatic.

My mother, bless her heart, proved me wrong.

India's Sons

1. Agence Presse France, "Indian Minister Says Rape 'Sometimes Right, Sometimes Wrong'," 6 June 2014, http://www.hurriyetdailynews.com/india-minister-says-rape-sometimes-right-sometimes-wrong-67486.

2. Ibid.

3. Abhinav Garg, "Defence Lawyers Blame Nirbhaya for Rape," *Times of India*, 4 March 2015, https://timesofindia.indiatimes.com/india/Defence-lawyers-blame-Nirbhaya-for-rape/articleshow/46451407.cms.

4. "Tehelka Stings Exposé: The Rapes Will Go On." YouTube, 7 April 2012, https://www.youtube.com/watch?v=jqlz0795gUg.

What Is Dark in Me Illumine

1. Although he pled no contest to the abuse, Gattani would go on to serve only thirty days in jail. Michael Daly, "Silicon Valley CEO Pleads 'No Contest' to Abusing His Wife and Is Offered a Deal for Less Than Thirty Days in Jail," *Daily Beast*, 17 April 2017, https://www.thedailybeast.com/silicon-valley-ceo-pleads-no-contest-to-abusing-his-wifeand-is-offered-a-deal-for-less-than-30-days-in-jail.

Some Ways to Disappear Girls in Salem, Tamil Nadu

1. Uma Girish, "Infanticide of Girls and Sex-Selective Abortion in India," Catholic Online, 21 February 2008, https://www.catholic.org/news/international/asia/story.php?id=26919.

Agnostic

1. At least we were in high school. If you were in middle school, you had to go to morning chapel.
2. Rick Paulas, "What Happened to Doomsday Prophet Harold Camping After the World Didn't End," *Vice*, 7 November 2014, https://www.vice.com/en_us/article/yvqkwb/life-after-doomsday-456.
3. And presumably gave up all your worldly goods and moved to a desert to await the end of the world.
4. Caitlin Dickinson, "Harold Camping Spent Around $100 Million on Rapture Ads," the *Atlantic*, 24 May 2011, https://www.theatlantic.com/national/archive/2011/05/harold-camping-spent-100-million-on-rapture-ads/351034/.
5. "Who Is Gurmeet Ram Rahim Singh?", Al Jazeera, 28 August 2017, https://www.aljazeera.com/indepth/features/2017/08/gurmeet-ram-rahim-singh-170827103334735.html
6. Roger Baird, "India's Controversial 'Bling Guru' Charged with Forcibly Castrating 400 Followers," 1 February 2018, https://www.ibtimes.co.uk/indias-controversial-bling-guru-charged-forcibly-castrating-400-followers-1658154.

The Aunty Problem

1. Marissa, *having taken three trains, a bus, and a car to get to Ryan's apartment*: Hello, Ryan!
    Ryan: Oh, uh, hi, Marissa.
    Pregnant pause
    Marissa: Ryan, I just wanted to say that you were right about that thing you said.
    Ryan: Oh.

Cinematic tension
Marissa: Okay. Well, uh, bye.
Marissa leaves, the entire scene having lasted about two minutes
Me: Girl, you couldn't have texted that?

2. We're talking completely deserted. Desolate. It was an old playground that had long since been left to crows and tumbleweed, and there were no houses near it. Besides, it was siesta time in Kerala: nobody did anything between 2 P.M. and 4 P.M.

Homely

1. As a Cancerian, I told myself that I was extremely homely. I loved never leaving my house. But apparently, it was not enough to lounge at home. You had to have a deep and abiding love for housework, which strikes me as a cruel and unnecessary thing to ask of any woman.

2. Or dies. But at least she dies next to a weeping man. Vindicated in the next life, if not in this one.

3. The modern Indian man might be more comfortable with his wife joining the workforce ("it doubles our incomes!") but considering that he still expects her to rise at 5 A.M. to pack lunches for him and the kids, this is a mixed blessing.

4. Not the kind of mad where they could be committed to an institution but certainly the kind of mad that made them prone to saying blurry things at the dinner table. Driblets of madness hung in the air around them—but it was acceptable for men to be a certain level of wine-soaked, sad, angry mad.

5. When I read these lines in the Bible, I remember thinking "that sounds like an awful lot for a woman to fit into her day." Meanwhile, all her husband has to do is "sitteth among the elders of the land."

6. A truly open mind—as Terry Pratchett once observed—is an incredibly attractive and rare thing. By "an open mind," I mean the kind of person you could go to if you ever had an alien encounter. They wouldn't call the police or humor you, they'd kind of nod and say thoughtfully, "Hmm, well, I didn't think

aliens were real, but I guess anything's possible in the world, isn't it?"

Why I'm No Longer Talking to White People about Arranged Marriage

1. Because Fate is invested in making us look foolish, you always end up doing the things you swear you would never do. If you hate the name Barry, guess what the love of your life's name will be.
2. As if being trapped in a house with twenty-five men isn't the stuff of horror movies.
3. OK, I'm making this up, but I will bet a lifetime supply of canned goods that somebody online asked it.
4. The groom might not turn up; it might rain; somebody might drop the cake; a wedding guest might wear a white dress; a relative might get drunk (Uncle Jeremy); the groom might forget his vows; somebody might propose to his girlfriend during the wedding (this actually happened in a "Dear Prudence" column!), etc.
5. One of the ceremonies—the mehendi—is exclusively for women to gossip, drink, sing vulgar songs, and get their hands painted with henna. It's a surefire stress cure for any young bride.
6. Indian weddings don't give the bride and groom a lot of time together, under the assumption that they have the rest of their lives for that.
7. I know this because several uncles had already made ribald jokes under the influence. "Do you want to hear a non-vegetarian joke?" they whispered lustily into each other's ears.

The Story of an Air Conditioner

1. And yet the number one topic of conversation at most dinners is: "Mira, I just can't seem to find any good help these days. Our *kaamwali bai* has the nerve to get sick without notice. I mean, that's just not done. I'm telling you, you have to be strict with these people. They're sly by nature. If you start to get lenient,

they take so much advantage of you, asking for holidays and whatnot—"

"Rita, you forget that, yaar. You have no idea what my girl is like! You're lucky. Mine is absolutely shameless, I tell you. She has the nerve to sass back when I tell her she has to stay late. 'I can't stay late every night,' that creature actually said. Imagine? And it's not as if it's every night—just the last few weeks—"

2. When I first heard the voices of people like Tracy Chapman, I couldn't believe they were women. I was so accustomed to women sounding pretty-pretty and precious when they sang. We are so afraid of women being real.

3. I have been most attracted to people when they are being visibly efficient: rolling Js, opening wine bottles, driving fast and well, packaging boxes, and so on. Competence is sexy. (It's just as well that most men are incompetent at small household tasks.)

Acknowledgments

Thank you to all the people who made this book possible. To dream editor, Radhika Marwah, for believing in it before it existed. To everyone at Penguin Random House who had a hand in designing and making *Besharam* real.

All that I know about bravery, I owe to my friends. To Apurva Kanak, fiercest heart in a small package. To Uvika Wahi, toughest wanderer.

To Salman Aldukheil: ten years is nothing on our friendship timeline. To my Twitter friends across the world—you make online bearable. More than bearable, delightful. Thank you for the memes and the lessons.

To all the women writers who have inspired me. To Arundhati Roy, Sylvia Plath, Toni Morrison, and Charlotte Brontë for being extraordinary women in any time and place.

To my brother, Alok, for being the good kid in the family. (Please never become an artist.)

To all my Delhi girlfriends—you know who you are. Thank you for being unapologetically yourself in a city that has never been easy on women.